OSPREY COMBAT AIRCRA

CONFLICT
IN THE BALKANS
1991–2000

SERIES EDITOR: TONY HOLMES

OSPREY COMBAT AIRCRAFT • 24

CONFLICT IN THE BALKANS
1991–2000

Tim Ripley

OSPREY
AVIATION

FRONT COVER
On 10 September 1995, at the height of the NATO air operation to force the lifting of the siege of Sarajevo, two RAF BAe Harrier GR7s of No.4 Squadron attacked a Bosnian Serb Army communications mast near Tuzla, in north east Bosnia, inflicting decisive damage. An RAF Jaguar of No.6 Squadron designated the Paveway II laser-guided bombs dropped by the Harriers using a TIALD pod. The target mast had already been heavily damaged by French Air Force Jaguars who dropped the main mast, and the RAF completed the attack against the secondary targets.

First published in Great Britain in 2001 by Osprey Publishing
Elms Court, Chapel Way, Botley, Oxford, OX2 9LP, UK
E-mail: info@ospreypublishing.com

© 2001 Osprey Publishing Limited

ISBN 1 84176 290 3

Series editor Tony Holmes
Page design and map by TT Designs, T & B Truscott
Cover Artwork by Keith Woodcock
Aircraft Profiles by Mark Rolfe
Index by Alan Thatcher
Origination by Grasmere Digital Imaging, Leeds, UK
Printed through Bookbuilders, Hong Kong

01 02 03 04 05   10 9 8 7 6 5 4 3 2 1

EDITOR'S NOTE
To make this best-selling series as authoritative as possible, the Editor would be interested in hearing from any individual who may have relevant photographs, documentation or first-hand experiences relating to combat, and the crews that flew them, in the various theatres of war. Any material used will be credited to its original source. Please write to Tony Holmes at 10 Prospect Road, Sevenoaks, Kent, TN13 3UA, Great Britain, or by e-mail at tony.holmes@osprey-jets.freeserve.co.uk

For a catalogue of all Osprey Publishing titles please contact us at:

Osprey Direct UK, P.O. Box 140, Wellingborough, Northants NN8 4ZA, UK
E-mail: **info@ospreydirect.co.uk**

**Osprey Direct USA,
c/o Motorbooks International, 729 Prospect Avenue, PO Box 1, Osceola, Wisconsin WI 54020**
E-mail: **info@ospreydirectusa.com**

Or visit our website: **www.ospreypublishing.com**

CONTENTS

INTRODUCTION

The politics behind the break-up of the former Socialist Federal Republic of Yugoslavia in the summer of 1991 are long and complex. There were a number of distinct conflicts during the period from 1991 to the end of 1999. The first was the Slovenian war of independence in June-July 1991, followed by the Croat-Serb conflict of 1991-92. This battle front remained largely quiet until the spring of 1995 when the Croats launched a decisive series of offensives. Then in April 1992 Bosnia-Herzegovina was engulfed in war between rival Serb, Croat and Muslim forces. United Nations (UN) peacekeeping troops and NATO airpower intervened in this three sided conflict from the summer of 1992 onwards, but with little impact until the autumn of 1995. The November 1995 Dayton Peace Accords and the Erdut Agreement formally ended the wars in both Bosnia and Croatia. This opened the way for NATO peacekeeping troops to enter the Balkans and separate the warring factions in Bosnia. The NATO-led Implementation Force (IFOR) and Stablisation Force (SFOR) achieved their limited military tasks with ease. Dayton, however, ignored the problem of ethnic Albanians, or Kosovars, living in the Serbian controlled province of Kosovo. A hint of trouble in the southern Balkans came in 1997 when Albania collapsed into turmoil, necessitating the deployment of an Italian-led European peacekeeping force. Tension in Kosovo led to war in 1998 and NATO intervention the following spring.

Airpower played a significant part in all these conflicts. This study looks specifically at air operations in the Balkans between 1991 and the summer of 2000. Since the summer of 1992 NATO air forces have been involved continuously in Balkan operations, with almost every squadron from the major west European air forces seeing service in the region at one time or another. A high proportion of US Air Force, Navy and Marine Corps aviation units have also pulled Balkan duty over the past decade. While the political and military impact of western air operations in the region are the subject of great debate, there is no doubt that the pilots and aircrews involved have repeatedly had to fly into harm's way with great skill and determination. NATO and UN airpower has been used in every conceivable type of operation, from strategic bombing by B-2 stealth bombers to air-to-air combat, moving ground troops by helicopter, to 'food bombing' for refugees trapped in Bosnian enclaves. The aircrews who maintained the Sarajevo airlift between 1992 and 1995 in the face of repeated targeting of their slow moving transport aircraft deserve particular praise. Even braver were the British Royal Navy and French Army Light Aviation (ALAT) helicopter crews who flew daring rescue missions to bring out both civilians from the besieged Bosnian town of Srebrenica in March and April 1993. They courageously pressed on in the face of Serb artillery fire to pluck to safety civilians and UN peacekeepers.

European peace envoy Carl Bildt called the former Yugoslavia 'Europe's Vietnam'. Only when peace is at last brought to the Balkans will the final chapter be written on the use of airpower in the region.

PART 1: THE FALL OF YUGOSLAVIA 1991-95

1991 YUGOSLAVIA AT WAR

Serbian strongman Slobodan Milosevic and the Federal Yugoslav military (JNA) high command reacted swiftly to the Slovenian declaration of independence in June 1991 with a massive military intervention. Slovenian Territorial Defence Force units were well prepared for the insurrection and pre-empted Yugoslav attempts to take control of their republic. Territorial Defence Force troops and local police seized key points around the country and besieged Federal military units in their garrisons. In the early evening of 27 June a Federal Yugoslav Air Force (JRV) SA-341 Gazelle carrying a cargo of bread was trying to find a landing site at a blockaded JNA barracks in the Slovenian capital Ljubljana, when a heat-seeking SA-7 Strella missile zoomed up from a city street. The helicopter exploded in mid air, showering the city with hot burning debris. This was the first aircraft to be lost in action during the bloody break up of Yugoslavia.

Milosevic's JNA tank columns were already heading into the small country, with the intention of seizing border crossing points. JRV ground attack aircraft, including Soko J-1 Jastrebs, G-4M Super Galebs, J-22 Oraos, MiG-21s and MiG-29s, swooped ahead of the ground troops, attacking civil aircraft at Ljubljana airport and border posts on the Austrian and Italian frontiers. Mil Mi-8 transport helicopters and Gazelles landed small parties of airborne troops ahead in vain attempts to seize key points. The Slovenian Territorial Defence Force was well armed, trained

Former Yugoslav Air Force and civilian Antonov An-2 light aircraft were pressed into service by the Croats to serve in liaison, casualty evacuation and ground attack roles (31st FWPA)

7

and motivated. Its volunteer militiamen held their ground, cut off the Federal troops' supply lines and then waited for them to surrender. By 7 July the Federal authorities threw in the towel and agreed to a European Economic Community (EEC) peace effort. Slovenia was free.

CROATIA

Attention now switched to Croatia, Yugoslavia's second largest and richest republic. Milosevic and his Serb nationalist supporters were not going to let it go without a serious fight. The JRV was in a state of crisis because of the Croat 'war of barracks' campaign, which saw thousands of Federal troops besieged in their garrisons throughout Croatia. By the autumn it had managed to pull back enough men and equipment to bases in Bosnia (Bihac, Banja Luka, Tuzla and Sarajevo) and into Serbia (Novi Sad, Vrasc and Sombor), as well as Udbina in the Serb occupied so-called Krajina region of Croatia, to begin operations in earnest against the Croats.

In September 1991 a state of open war existed between Croatia and Serbia along a 1,000 mile front, with the JRV striking at targets deep inside Croatia. MiG-21s made sweeps over the Croat capital Zagreb and, on 7 October, launched a very precise attack on the Presidential Palace with infra-red guided AGM-65 Maverick missiles believed to have been fired from a MiG-29. Croatian President Franjo Tudjman was only a few feet away from the impact area but survived.

The main emphasis of the JRV offensive was in Eastern Slavonia, where Croat troops were putting up strong resistance to Serb offensives across the Danube. From August onwards, JRV jets made daily strikes against

Many Croatian air force aircraft, such as the Antonov An-32 were given civilian registrations and colour schemes to disguise their origins and protect Zagreb's covert arms purchasing operations in breach of the UN arms embargo *(Tim Ripley)*

A casualty evacuation configured Antonov An-2 unloads its cargo of wounded soldiers at Zagreb's Pleso Airport in July 1992 (Tim Ripley)

the city of Vukovar, which became known as the 'Stalingrad of the Balkans'. It held out for 100 days until the starved defenders surrendered in November. Serb soldiers then shot hundreds of their prisoners. Some 46 JRV aircraft and helicopters were lost in the bloody conflicts with Slovenia and Croatia.

The JRV's lamentable air campaign culminated on 7 January 1992 with the shooting down of a white-painted and unarmed Italian Army Bell-Agusta 205, serving with the European Community Monitoring Mission, by a MiG-21, over Croatia. The five crew and observers on the helicopter were killed.

CROAT AIRPOWER

Newly independent Croatia had found itself without an air force in the summer of 1991, after the JRV spirited away almost all its aircraft back to safety in Bosnia and Serbia. The Croat paramilitary Special Police had a small air arm with a handful of Bell 206 and 212 helicopters, along with a couple of Mi-8s. A handful of MiG-21 pilots of Croat origin defected from the JRV with their aircraft, but some were soon lost in action. Lacking modern munitions, the new Croat Air Force (HRZ) had to resort to rough and ready improvisations to take the war to the Serbs. Antonov An-2 bi-planes were press-ganged from parachute clubs into military service, first dropping supplies to besieged Vukovar and then becoming bombers. Recycled explosives were then used to fill old oil drums or gas cylinders to create Croatia's first indigenously manufactured air launched ordnance. It is not thought that the improvised weapons killed many Serbs but they certainly raised morale among the Croats.

The Serb-Croat war burnt itself out in the spring of 1992 and an uneasy peace reigned for three years under the supervision of the UN Protection Force. A third of the territory of the old Croat republic was now held by Serb forces. Under the terms of the cease fire the JNA was supposed to withdraw from Croat territory, but it simply handed its weapons over to locally recruited militia forces of the newly declared Republic of Serb Krajina. The Croats used this time to rebuild their army and air force, buying more than 20 MiG-21s, 40 Mi-8s and 15 Mil Mi-24 attack helicopters on the international arms black market. The Croat aviation industry was pressed into service to build up the country's air power, including the design and fielding of a family of unmanned air vehicles (UAVs). By the spring of 1995 the Croats were ready to strike.

The Croatian military and aviation industry jointly created a family of unmanned air vehicles that saw extensive service in the run-up to and during Operation Storm in July and August 1995

BOSNIAN WAR 1992-95

Since the start of the war in Croatia, tension had been rising in Bosnia as the republic's Serb population demanded the right to their own independent state. How much of this was on the prompting of hardline nationalists from Belgrade is unclear, but by April 1992 the Bosnian Serbs had armed their population with ex-JNA weapons and were ready to take on the predominately Muslim regime in Sarajevo and their nominal Croat allies. The declaration of independence from Yugoslavia by the Sarajevo government in April 1992 was the spark that ignited the war. Soon Serb para-military forces were rampaging through the country expelling hundreds of thousands to create ethnically pure regions. The self-declared Republika Srpska, or Serb Republic, soon set up its own armed forces to defend the 1,000 mile long front from Muslim and Croat forces. The VRS (Bosnian Serb Army) set up its own air force, with JRV (Federal Yugoslav Air Force) help, at Banja Luka in May 1992. It was soon in action helping Bosnian Serb Army units defeat Muslim and Croat forces to open the Possavina Corridor linking Yugoslavia with Serb held areas of Bosnia around Banja Luka.

The hard pressed Bosnian government forces soon pressed a number of light aircraft into service to supply their beleaguered enclaves. Black-market purchases of Mil Mi-8 helicopters from Eastern European sources helped this effort and, for the next three years, Bosnian and mercenary pilots continued to fly dare-devil missions behind Serb lines to keep Muslim forces fighting in the face of overwhelming odds.

Boeing E-3A Sentry AWACS radar surveillance aircraft of the NATO Airborne Early Warning Force started patrols over the Balkans in the spring of 1992 and have been on duty in the region ever since (DASA)

This Aerospatiale AS 332 Super Puma flew into Sarajevo in June 1992 carrying French President François Mitterrand's party but it was damaged at the airport and had to be dismantled before it could be removed back to France on a C-130 (ECPA)

WESTERN INTERVENTION

NATO air forces first became involved in the former Yugoslavia in the summer of 1992, when the Alliance decided to dispatch a naval embargo force to the Adriatic Sea to enforce the United Nations arms embargo against all the republics that used to form the Socialist Federal Republic of Yugoslavia. The air component of this operation consisted of Boeing E-3A Sentry AWACS radar surveillance aircraft of the multi-national NATO Airborne Early Warning Force to provide top cover for Alliance ships.

Meanwhile the Bosnian capital was being besieged by Serb forces and its citizens bombarded by artillery positioned in the hills surrounding the city. For two months battles raged around the city between government forces and Bosnian Serb Army troops. A small UN contingent was trapped in the city and eventually it managed to negotiate a deal to allow them to take control of the airport on the eastern suburbs so a humanitarian airlift could be started. The airlift was prompted by concern that the besieged citizens of Sarajevo could soon face starvation.

For several days the airlift was stalled until French President François Mitterrand made a daring flight into the city on 28 June on board a Eurocopter AS365 Dauphin helicopter, of the French *Armée de l'Air* ET60 VIP transport unit. The day after, on the personal orders of Mitterrand,

German *Luftwaffe* C.160 Transalls on the packed flight line at Zagreb in July 1992, which had become the main hub for the UNHCR airbridge to Sarajevo *(Tim Ripley)*

This Antonov An-12 aircraft was one of the first East European transport aircraft to be chartered by the UN Protection Force. It started flying shuttle flights to Sarajevo from UN logistic bases in Zagreb and Belgrade in July 1992 *(Tim Ripley)*

A cargo of humanitarian aid is unloaded from a USAF Lockheed C-130E Hercules by French *Armée de l'Air* ground personnel in the first days of the Sarajevo airlift in July 1992 *(Tim Ripley)*

two French C.160 Transall transport aircraft landed at Sarajevo to kick-start the airlift. Not wishing to be outdone by the French, other air forces were ordered to send transport aircraft to Sarajevo with relief supplies. American, Belgian, British, Canadian, German, Greek, Italian, Saudi Arabian and Turkish aircraft were soon flying daily shuttle flights to Sarajevo from bases around Europe, although by mid-July most of the aircraft committed to the airlift were staging through Zagreb.

The UN High Commissioner for Refugees (UNHCR) European headquarters in Geneva provided the overall co-ordination for the airlift. Sarajevo airport itself was soon operating under *Armée de l'Air* control on behalf of the UN. Canadian troops at first were assigned to guard the airport until they were replaced by French forces later in the summer. During the summer some 20 flights a day were being made into the airport, which was now situated across a very active frontline. Aircraft were regularly shot at and, on several occasions, the UN closed down the airlift when heavy fighting broke out near the airport or under the glide path.

Tragedy struck on 3 September 1992, when an Italian Air Force Alenia G222 transport was hit and brought down on its final approach to

The USAF and Canadian Forces donated large cargo handling tractors to the UNHCR in Sarajevo to speed up the unloading of aid pallets from aircraft, reducing the time they had to remain exposed on the parking pan at Sarajevo *(Tim Ripley)*

Aircrew flying into Sarajevo all wore body armour to protect themselves from hostile fire. Aircraft were also fitted with kevlar armour and self protection systems to defeat hostile anti-aircraft missiles *(Tim Ripley)*

Sarajevo airport, killing the four crew aboard. A combat search and rescue mission by US Marine Corps Bell AH-1W Cobras and Sikorsky CH-53Es was fired upon as it approached the crash site. To date no one has claimed responsibility for the attack on the Italian aircraft, although it occurred above an area contested by all three sides in the conflict. The result of the attack was to close down the airlift for a month. The USAF re-opened the airbridge on 3 October and, within days, British, Canadian, French and German aircraft joined the effort with transport aircraft equipped with missile self defence systems. Day in and day out for the next three years, UNHCR aircraft flew into the airport, in spite of its terrible weather, minimal navigation aids and the constant danger of being shot at in the air and on the ground. The UNHCR airbridge kept the city of Sarajevo fed through three more winters, with some 12,951 flights being flown into the city until the

The view from the cockpit of a USAF Lockheed C-130E Hercules on the final approach to Sarajevo airport *(Tim Ripley)*

operation finally came to an end in January 1996. Some 270 aircraft were shot at in this period, with some 50 aircraft taking hits from ground fire. No aircraft were lost apart from the Italian G.222 and a chartered Ilyushin Il-76 that skidded off the runway after a poor landing.

SREBRENICA 1993

International peace efforts produced little during the final months of 1992, and fighting flared around a string of Muslim-held enclaves in eastern Bosnia. Cut off for months, the enclaves around Srebrenica, Zepa and Gorazde were desperately short of food and medical supplies. The French commander of the UN Protection Force's Bosnia-Herzegovina Command, Major General Philippe Morillon, managed to bluff his way into Srebrenica and found the situation desperate, with more than 25,000 people existing in near medieval conditions.

The USAF was ordered by US President Bill Clinton to mount Operation Provide Promise to air-drop humanitarian aid to the enclaves from its massive base at Rhein-Main, near Frankfurt in Germany. Beginning on 28 February 1993, USAF Lockheed C-130E Hercules

Rhein-Main AB in Germany was the hub for USAF participation in the UNHCR airbridge to Sarajevo and the aid airdrops to the eastern enclaves. At the height of operations in 1993 and 1994, some 44 Lockheed C-130 Hercules aircraft were deployed at the base (Tim Ripley)

Dutch Air Force Lockheed Martin F-16A Fighting Falcon aircraft of 315 Squadron flew some of the first mission of Operation Deny Flight to impose the No Fly Zone over Bosnia *(US DoD/JCC(D))*

The USAF deployed its top air superiority fighter, the McDonnell Douglas F-15C Eagle, to Aviano AB in Italy to lead its participation in Operation Deny Flight *(US DoD/JCC(D))*

US Navy McDonnell Douglas F/A-18C Hornets based on the carrier USS *Theodore Roosevelt* flew swing role missions – air supremacy and close air support – over Bosnia in the summer of 1993 *(Tim Ripley)*

aircraft made nightly supply drops to the enclaves. Formations of up to nine aircraft at a time would make night time forays over eastern Bosnia on a regular basis for almost eighteen months. In early 1994, the airdrop and airlift effort was stepped-up with more than 44 Hercules aircraft, including a strong contingent from the USAF Reserve and Air National

Guard, being deployed by the Americans to Rhein-Main, along with French and German C.160 aircraft. During the air-drop operation, the Americans progressed from dropping wooden pallets of aid to creating 'food cluster bombs' out of large cardboard cartons, which broke open near the ground, scattering US military rations food packets over the drop zone. By the time the last air drops were made in August 1994, when the Bosnian Serb Army activated their radar guided surface-to-air missile defence system over Bosnia, some 2,828 sorties had been flown.

The crisis over Srebrenica was not resolved until April 1993 when the UN declared the enclave a demilitarised 'safe area' and deployed Canadian peacekeeping troops to protect it. The UN then attempted to open an air evacuation route to Srebrenica to bring out the hundreds of wounded people in the enclave in March. On 24 March French Army Light Aviation (ALAT) Aerospatiale SA.330 Pumas and British Royal Navy Westland Sea King HC.4 helicopters made their first flight into Srebrenica. The French helicopters were shelled as they took off from the improvised landing zone. Several UN soldiers were injured and two Sea Kings flew in to bring them out. The British helicopters were also shelled but they managed

French *Aeronautique Navale* Westland Lynx HAS 4(FR) carried boarding parties to inspect cargo ships in the Adriatic suspected of breaching the UN arms embargo against all the former Yugoslav republics *(Tim Ripley)*

USAF Boeing KC-135 Stratotankers were essential to making Operation Deny Flight work, refuelling allied fighters en route to patrol the no-fly zone over Bosnia *(Tim Ripley)*

The air supremacy version of the Dassault Mirage 2000, the C model, were the first French *Armée de l'Air* aircraft to be deployed to Italy to participate in Operation Deny Flight *(US DoD/JCC(D))*

to fly out the casualties to safety at Tuzla. The UN controlled airport in the northern Bosnian city was then shelled as the wounded were being unloaded from the helicopters.

CRISIS MANAGEMENT

The continuing escalation of the Bosnian conflict in the autumn of 1992 had forced the international community to increase its 'crisis management' efforts to contain and limit the war. In October 1992, the UN imposed a 'no-fly zone' for military aircraft over Bosnia, and the NATO Airborne Early Warning Force extended its scope of operations to include monitoring of this zone, with E-3 aircraft in tracks over the Adriatic and Hungary. The latter move was the first time NATO air forces had operated over the territory of a former Warsaw Pact state. Bosnia's warring factions showed total disregard for the UN no-fly zone, and amid the Srebrenica crisis in March 1993 it was agreed by the UN Security Council that NATO airpower would be used to enforce the flight ban. American, British, Dutch, French and Turkish fighter aircraft were moved to Italy, or based on aircraft carriers in the Adriatic, to work under the command of NATO's 5th Allied Tactical Air Force (5ATAF) to enforce the no-fly zone. On 12 April 1993, NATO aircraft began Operation Deny Flight which saw around the clock fighter combat air patrols over Bosnia to stop the warring factions using combat aircraft.

The fighters' operations were controlled by very strict rules of engagement to prevent any 'politically' damaging incidents, so only aircraft actively engaged in combat missions could be engaged by the NATO aircraft; other aircraft or helicopters could only be warned to land and buzzed at high speed to force them to land. While the warring factions made great use of helicopters for resupply missions, they generally did not employ their fighter aircraft during 1993 and into 1994.

The vulnerability of UN peacekeeping troops to reprisals by local forces made the issue of air strikes the subject of much political infighting in the world's capitals, with the US keen to use airpower and the Europeans more cautious. Stuck in the middle of this high level political dogfight were the troops of the UN Protection Force and the airmen of NATO's 5 ATAF. In June 1993, the international community agreed to provide the UN Protection Force with close air support if its troops came

Bosnian Croat HVO militia used Mil Mi-8 helicopters to resupply their enclaves in central Bosnia besieged by government forces during the bloody Muslim-Croat conflict
(Tim Ripley)

under attack, so 5 ATAF was allowed to start flying close air support aircraft over Bosnia on a daily basis to be ready to strike if UN troops came under fire, but only if the UN Secretary General, or his nominated representative, agreed. This became known as the so-called 'dual key' arrangement. Just a month later NATO's new strike capability was used to issue an ultimatum to the Bosnian Serb Army to withdraw from Mount Igman overlooking Sarajevo.

Airbases in Italy became home to a steady stream of NATO squadrons as allied air forces began a rotation of units through Operation Deny Flight duty. Most squadron detachments spent between two and three months on duty in Italy, flying daily missions over Bosnia, either chasing no-fly zone violators or practising close air support procedures with UN tactical air control parties on the ground. During the autumn, NATO aircraft began to be called into action to provide what was termed an 'air presence' over UN troops who were being threatened by hostile troops. Usually the appearance of heavily armed Fairchild A-10A Warthogs or SEPECAT Jaguars forced Bosnian 'warlords' to back down and allow the UN to continue with their humanitarian mission.

Lockheed P-3 Orions from several allied air forces deployed to Sigonella on Sicily to patrol the Adriatic for embargo busting ships under the code-name Operation Sharp Guard. This is a Portuguese Air Force P-3P Orion *(Tim Ripley)*

SARAJEVO 1994

By the end of 1993, international intervention in Bosnia seemed to have run into a dead-end. All the peace plans had failed and the warring factions were showing no sign of wearying of fighting. A mortar attack in Sarajevo in early February 1994 that left 68 civilians dead finally galvanised western political leaders to take a more 'robust' attitude to the Bosnian issue. The UN's new commander in Sarajevo, Britain's Lieutenant General Sir Michael Rose, was able to capitalise on this new mood after NATO issued an ultimatum threatening air strikes if the warring factions did not move all their heavy weapons out of

Royal Air Force Panavia Tornado F3 fighters patrolled the no-fly zone during Operation Deny Flight from Gioia del Colle AB in southern Italy for two and a half years from April 1993 *(Tim Ripley)*

a 20 mile exclusion zone around the city or place them under UN control. At the last minute, after the arrival of Russian troops, the Serbs backed down and pulled their guns back. This set the agenda for the coming year, with a series of crises developing around Sarajevo over the control of Serb heavy weapons. Twice during the summer Rose called in air strikes against weapons not in control points around the Bosnian capital.

UN Antonov An-32 transport aircraft flew regular supply missions around the former Yugoslavia, including many missions into Sarajevo *(UN)*

SHOOT DOWN, FEBRUARY 1994

On 28 February 1994, the 86th Wing's 526th 'Black Knights' Fighter Squadron arrived at Aviano with their Block 40 F-16s to take over NATO duty just as the alliance and the UN were locked into a stand-off with Serb forces around Sarajevo, after a mortar round had killed dozens of people in a market. Three weeks later the squadron played a key role in the shooting down of four Serb aircraft.

In the space of that short engagement, Captain Bob 'Wilbur' Wright, earned the status of the USAF's highest scoring F-16 pilot. At the time, for operational security reasons the USAF refused to identify Wright publicly because he was still flying missions over Bosnia as part of NATO's Operation Deny Flight. It was several months before he was named when the then Lockheed Fort Worth Company, the F-16 makers, presented him with the Dryen Semper Viper Award, for 'superior airmanship'.

The deadly engagement began just after 5.30 am on 24 February 1994, when a NATO AWACS aircraft detected a flight of six fast jets heading southwards from Banja Luka towards central Bosnia. It later transpired that the SOKO G-2 Galeb aircraft had taken off from Udbina airbase in the Serb held Krajina region in Croatia. Wright and his then wingman, a little known Captain Scott O'Grady, were on combat air patrol over Mostar, in south east Bosnia, using the callsigns Black 03 and 04. They were then serving with the 526th FS, which had been detached for temporary duty to Aviano from Ramstein. A fighter controller on the AWACS vectored the two pilots to intercept the Serb aircraft. At the same time, the E-3A began issuing radio warnings to the Serbs, ordering them to land or exit the UN mandated no-fly zone otherwise they would be engaged. They did not respond to the warnings.

At 5.42am, Wright and O'Grady issued their own warnings to the Serbs, which were also ignored. This was just after Wright had seen the Serb aircraft make bombing runs on an arms factory in the Muslim held town of Novi Travnik. Wright saw explosions on the ground and requested permission from NATO's Combined Air Operations Centre at Vicenza to engage. Under the UN and NATO rules of engagement, NATO had a 'single key' in such circumstances, so the Combined Air Operations Centre was almost immediately able to clear Wright to react to this blatant breach of the no-fly zone.

The Galebs were now heading northwards, trying to drop to low level

19

to use the mountainous terrain to hide from any NATO radar surveillance. Wright, however, was on their tail. At 5.45am he launched his first AIM-120 Advanced Medium Range Air-to-Air Missile (AMRAAM) at the Galebs. The semi-active radar guided missile easily found its mark on the first Galeb, which was flying at some 5,000 feet. Now the remaining Galebs had dropped to a few hundred feet to make their escape back to Udbina. Wright pressed on, closing to within AIM-9 Sidewinder range. He loosed off two of the heat-seeking missiles. They were seen to impact and turn the Serb aircraft into fireballs. No parachutes were seen by the F-16 pilots.

With his missiles all but exhausted and his fuel running low, Wright now handed over the chase to O'Grady, who had been flying top cover for his flight lead. O'Grady dropped down to engage and fired a Sidewinder but it did not lock-on and missed. Black Flight was now approaching 'bingo fuel' so they pulled off to refuel on from a Boeing KC-135R Stratotanker circling in an orbit over the Adriatic. Another pair of 526th FS F-16Cs, Knight 25 and 26, had been vectored to take over the intercept by the AWACS. At 5.50pm Knight 25 managed to get in behind the remaining three Galebs. He got a good lock and downed a Serb with a Sidewinder. By now the Serbs were close to the international border and the F-16s had to break off the pursuit because NATO was not empowered to engage aircraft outside Bosnian airspace. The Serb pilots were able to land safely at Udbina. Within minutes the news of the first offensive military action in the history of the NATO alliance was flashed around the world. Wright and his colleagues later gave a number of media interviews about the incident, using their 'callsigns' as a means of identification, but they quietly returned to operational flying.

The US established a Joint Special Operations Task Force at Brindisi, in southern Italy, in 1993 to provide combat search and rescue coverage for allied forces in the Balkans *(Paul Beaver)*

French Army Light Aviation (ALAT) Aerospatiale SA 341 Gazelles flew deep into Bosnia on some of the most dangerous missions of the war undertaken by western pilots *(Tim Ripley)*

Norwegian Air Force Bell 412SP Arapahos helicopters supported the UN Nordic Battalion in Bosnia from 1993 onwards under the code-name 'Nor Air' *(Tim Ripley)*

GORAZDE, APRIL 1994

With NATO and the UN now adopting a 'robust' approach both on the ground and in the air, international intervention in Bosnia at last looked as if it was making progress. A ceasefire and a peace plan of sorts were also starting to take shape. Even the Croats and Muslims had agreed to stop fighting each other and join forces against the Serbs. UN and NATO leadership, however, had not factored in the influence of Bosnian Serb Army commander General Ratko Mladic. He was not impressed by the peace plan or being told what to do by the UN, NATO or anyone else. In April he ordered his army to launch an all-out offensive to take the Gorazde enclave in eastern Bosnia. Apart from a small observer team and a British tactical air control party there were no UN units in the enclave and they were soon being targeted by Serb fire.

On the afternoon of 10 April, a pair of 512th FS F-16s were on patrol over Bosnia when a call for help came from British Special Air Service (SAS) troops under Serb tank fire in Gorazde. Directed by a Lockheed EC-130E Airborne Battlefield Command and Control Centre aircraft, the two F-16s tried to find the Serb tanks. Low cloud prevented them finding their primary target so the British SAS tactical air control party redirected them to a secondary target, an artillery command post. In 'marginal' weather the F-16s put four 500lb Mk.82 bombs on target, temporarily holding up the Serb advance. The Bosnian Serb Army attacks continued the following day and a pair of US Marine Corps McDonnell Douglas F/A-18As, VMFA-(AW)-251, carried out a repeat attack.

21

The first ever air strikes by NATO aircraft temporarily calmed the situation but within days the Serbs were attacking again. A French Etendard IV reconnaissance aircraft was hit by a heat-seeking missile while over the enclave, and a British BAe Sea Harrier FRS.1 was shot down while making repeated passes trying to find close air support targets. The pilot ejected safely into Bosnian controlled territory and was later flown out of the enclave on a Det ALAT Split Puma, along with the SAS team.

With Serb forces poised to take Gorazde, NATO now imposed another weapon exclusion zone around the enclave and threatened heavy air strikes unless Mladic called off his attack. The Serb General blinked. UN troops entered the enclave in strength and the crisis passed. Bosnia's frontlines were now strangely quiet.

UDBINA, NOVEMBER 1994

International diplomatic efforts to broker a peace plan finally ran out of steam in the autumn. Heavy fighting was now breaking out in the north west of Bosnia, around the so-called Bihac pocket. Major infringements of the no-fly zone took place during November 1994 around Bihac, when Serb fighters based in Croatia were making brief dashes across the border to bomb Bosnian positions in the enclave. NATO fighters could not stop the Serb aircraft because the rules of engagement said they could not engage outside Bosnian airspace. A pair of RAF Tornado F3s were set to intercept a flight of Galebs but they were called off when the Serb aircraft crossed out of Bosnian airspace. The Croat Government was now threatening to intervene to save Bihac unless the UN and NATO did something. The American, British and French governments gave the green light for an attack to put Udbina airbase, the source of the Serb air strikes, out of action.

At 11.30am on 21 November a large multi-national NATO strike package took off to attack the airbase. USAF McDonnell Douglas F-15E Strike Eagles, USMC McDonnell Douglas F/A-18Ds and French SEPECAT Jaguars used laser-guided bombs against the airfield's runways, taxi-ways and air defences. USAF F-16s employed CBU-87

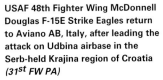

USAF 48th Fighter Wing McDonnell Douglas F-15E Strike Eagles return to Aviano AB, Italy, after leading the attack on Udbina airbase in the Serb-held Krajina region of Croatia *(31st FW PA)*

A French *Armée de l'Air* SEPECAT Jaguar A on close air support patrol over Bosnia armed with free-flight rocket pods *(Tim Ripley)*

Chartered Yakovlev Yak-40s were used to fly international diplomats and senior UN commanders around the former Yugoslavia *(Tim Ripley)*

cluster bombs to put more taxi-ways out of action and prevent repair teams clearing up the mess quickly.

Following the Udbina air strike and subsequent NATO attacks on Serb anti-aircraft sites in north-west Bosnia, the Serbs escalated the conflict by taking more than 300 UN troops hostage around Sarajevo. Western governments backed down and refused to call Mladic's bluff. NATO air operations were dramatically scaled down and the Bosnian Serb Army released their hostages.

CAT AND MOUSE 1995

Next spring a repeat of the hostage crisis occurred when the new UN commander in Bosnia, Lieutenant General Rupert Smith, ordered two NATO air strikes on a Serb weapons dump outside Sarajevo after they removed artillery from a UN collection point.

On 25 May USAF F-16s and Spanish EF-18A Hornets armed with Paveway laser-guided bombs attacked Bosnian Serb ammunition dumps south of Pale. This was the first time F-16 and EF-18 aircraft had used laser-guided bombs in anger. The attack did not induce a change of behaviour. The following day, Aviano based F-16s returned to inflict more destruction on the Pale ammunition storage complex. More than 400 UN peacekeepers were now taken hostage and more NATO airstrikes were now off the agenda.

Again the UN and NATO were ordered to back down by western

Royal Air Force Boeing Chinook HC2 helicopters provided the heavy lift component of the British Army's 24 Airmobile Brigade, which was a key player in the UN's Rapid Reaction Force *(Land Command Media Production Centre)*

31st Fighter Wing Lockheed Martin F-16C Block 40 Fighting Falcons equipped with LANTIRN pods were in the thick of the action during 1995 hitting a range of targets with laser-guided bombs *(Tim Ripley)*

governments in order to secure the release of the peacekeepers held hostage by the Serbs. During this crisis USAF Captain Scott O'Grady's F-16C was shot down by a Serb SA-6 SAM over western Bosnia. Further humiliation was heaped on the UN and NATO in July when their political masters called off air operations in support of the Dutch garrison defending the UN safe area at Srebrenica after UN troops were again taken hostage by the Serbs. A pair of Dutch F-16As made one successful attack but a follow-up wave of USAF F-16s could not find their targets. Serb forces soon entered the enclave. More than 6,000 Muslim prisoners were killed in mass executions by Mladic's men as Serb forces completed the ethnic cleansing of the enclave.

After the debacle at Srebrenica, UN and NATO commanders in the

US Navy and Marine Corps Grumman EA-6B Prowler electronic warfare aircraft supported every major allied air operation during 1995 to neutralise radar guided SAM threats *(Tim Ripley)*

Dutch Lockheed Martin F-16A Fighting Falcons of 322nd Squadron were heavily involved in strikes on Srebrenica in July 1995 and later during Operation Allied Force *(Tim Ripley)*

Balkans were given the go ahead by western governments at the July London Conference to begin preparations for widespread offensive air action against the Bosnian Serbs, if the remaining safe areas came under attack again. A key element was the delegation of the 'key' to launch air strikes from the UN political supremo in the Balkans, Yasushi Akashi, to the senior UN Peace Forces commander in Zagreb, French Lieutenant General Bernard Janvier and his NATO counterpart, Admiral Leighton 'Snuffy' Smith. Western leaders in effect set a 'trip wire' for air strikes.

In August 1995 the Croats struck back at the Serbs, seizing almost all the territory lost in the 1991 war. Operation Storm saw Croat Mi-8 helicopters deliver commandos behind enemy lines and Zagreb's MiG-21s flew scores of close air support and interdiction missions. Krajina and Bosnian Serb jets that tried to intervene suffered heavily to Croat air defences, losing two aircraft.

To clear the decks and prevent further hostage taking UN troops were withdrawn from the enclaves of Gorazde and Zepa in August. US peace envoy Richard Holbrooke began touring Europe in the last week of August to launch a major US peace initiative.

Ukrainian Army Aviation Mil Mi-26 transport helicopters were based at Split, Croatia, during the summer of 1995 to move humanitarian aid to Tuzla in northern Bosnia for thousands of Muslim refugees expelled from the Srebrenica safe area after its capture by Serb forces *(Tim Ripley)*

Croatian War Aviation Mikoyan MiG-21bis fighter bombers based at Pula, Split and Zagreb spearheaded the Operation Storm offensive that decisively defeated Serb forces in the Krajina region *(31st FW PA)*

The British Army Air Corps deployed Lynx AH.7s of 664 Squadron to Croatia in early 1995 to support the British UN contingent in Bosnia, providing a much needed rapid response armed helicopter and reconnaissance capability *(Tim Ripley)*

THE RELIEF OF SARAJEVO

The trigger for the unleashing of NATO airpower was a random mortar attack on Sarajevo on the morning of 28 August 1995 that left 37 civilians dead and scores wounded. Within hours NATO and the UN had completed preparations for a series of air strikes which would dramatically change the military balance in Bosnia. During the afternoon, Admiral Smith and General Smith, who had the UN 'bombing key' in the absence of General Janvier who was on holiday, both developed the plans for the UN-NATO response to the mortar attack. It was determined that the Serbs were the culprits for the mortar attack, and the major air response agreed at the London Conference would be executed. After General Smith ordered the small British garrison in Gorazde to make a dash for safety in Yugoslavia, he 'turned' the UN 'bombing key' and Admiral Smith did the same for NATO. Western governments now

Mil Mi-8 helicopters from Ukraine's Army Aviation were used to support UN troops in Croatia during the summer of 1995 *(Tim Ripley)*

For Operation Deliberate Force the USAF deployed a detachment of McDonnell Douglas KC-10 Extender tankers to Pisa Airport in Italy to dramatically increase NATO air-to-air refuelling capability *(Tim Ripley)*

Royal Navy Sea Kings of 845 Naval Air Squadron training to move the artillery of the UN Rapid Reaction Force *(Land Command Media Production Centre)*

had little choice but to back their military commanders. The clock was now ticking towards the launching of Operation Deliberate Force.

During 28 August, the Combined Air Operations Centre at Vicenza was making the necessary preparations to muster a force of more than 350 aircraft for the operation. Strike aircraft and tankers were recalled from home bases to Italy to allow the first strike to go in the early hours of 30 August. NATO's southern European air commander, USAF Lieutenant General Mike Ryan flew up to Vicenza on the morning of 29 August to take personal command of the operation. 5 ATAF was to execute the air plan in co-ordination with General Smith's UN forces, via the UN Rapid Reaction Force Operations Staff headquarters, which was based just outside Sarajevo at Kiseljak. At Vicenza, air planners under the Combined Air Operations Centre director, USAF Major Hal Hornburg, began to move into high gear to match weapons and aircraft to targets. Contingency plans for the air campaign were already at an advanced stage, but there was little time before the first bombs were to be dropped. All the details the NATO aircrews needed to conduct the air strikes were contained in 5 ATAF's air tasking message, which was faxed by secure communications and satellite links to NATO air bases in Italy, France, Germany and Britain and to aircraft carriers in the Adriatic Sea. The air armada was organised into a series of strike packages, which combined bomb-dropping or missile firing aircraft with fighters, suppression of enemy air defences aircraft, combat search and rescue support and air-to-air refuelling tankers, backed up by photographic reconnaissance aircraft. Each package contained aircraft drawn from several of the nations participating in the NATO operation.

Additional co-ordination was required with the UN Air Operations Co-ordination Centre in Sarajevo and the Rapid Reaction Force Operations Staff's Tactical Air Operations Centre to ensure that UN ground troops knew exactly what was happening and could keep away from any air strikes. USAF EC-130H airborne command post aircraft, with their extensive radio and satellite communications links, provided the real-time link between inbound NATO aircraft and tactical air control parties on the ground, who would direct a number of the strikes against targets in the Sarajevo area. The tactical air control parties would also call in any close air support aircraft if Serb artillery and mortars retaliated against UN troops.

DEAD-EYE SOUTH EAST

NATO aircraft started taking off late in the evening of 29 August, bound for their targets in eastern Bosnia. In the first phase of the operation, targets in the west of Bosnia were left alone. USAF KC-135 and McDonnell Douglas KC-10 Extender tankers were orbiting over the Adriatic near Split to refuel the first strike package of 14 suppression of enemy air defence (SEAD) and three strike aircraft. Armed with AGM-88 High Speed Anti-Radiation Missiles (HARMS) and Paveway laser-guided bombs, the Hornets, F-16s and Grumman EA-6B Prowlers had the mission to cripple the Serbs' integrated air defence network in eastern Bosnia. Under the code name Dead-Eye South East, the package hit 15 targets including surface-to-air missile batteries, communications sites, radar networks and command bunkers. Immediately prior to the strikes, US Navy aircraft released a swarm of AGM-141 Tactical Air Launched Decoys, in an attempt to get the Bosnian Serb Army air defences to switch on their radar network to allow the HARMs to home in on active radars. The Serbs maintained their discipline and refused to take the bait.

The span of the NATO attack stretched from Neveslaje, near Mostar, up to Bijelina near Tuzla. The first bombs landed just after 2am on 30 August on an SA-6 surface-to-air missile (SAM) battery north of Sarajevo. The main Serb air defence control bunker on Mount Jahorina, east of Sarajevo, received a heavy pounding to prevent any co-ordinated

AGM-88 HARM armed McDonnell Douglas F/A-18C Hornets flew constant patrols to respond to SAM threats against allied aircraft operating over Bosnia *(Tim Ripley)*

response by the Serb SAMs or anti-aircraft artillery. Support from radar jamming Grumman EF-111A Ravens and EC-130H Compass Call aircraft blinded any radars that remained in operation, as well any radio links between SAM batteries. Orbiting over the Adriatic were USAF RC-135 Rivet Joint electronic intelligence gathering aircraft, watching for any response from the Bosnian Serb Army air

Two-seat USMC McDonnell Douglas F/A-18D Hornets, of VMFA(AW)-533 brought a true multi-role capability to NATO operations during 1995, flying with AIM-9 Sidewinder air-to-air missiles, Paveway laser guided bombs and AGM-88 HARM anti-radar weapons *(Tim Ripley)*

defence network. Also in the air were a pair of close air support aircraft ready to respond to any Serb artillery fire, and a combat search and rescue package of USAF Special Operations Command Sikorsky MH-53J Pave Low III helicopters and HC-130 tankers. In the event, they were not required.

STRIKING SARAJEVO

One hour and 40 minutes after the Dead-Eye South East package had headed for home, its mission accomplished, NATO's 5ATAF sent the first of five strike packages of the day into action over Sarajevo. Code-named Sarajevo Strike Package Alpha, Bravo, Charlie, Delta and Echo, these packages attacked specific targets, such as ammunition dumps, communications sites and repair bases, with laser-guided bombs. Each raid lasted between 20 and 30 minutes.

Television cameras filmed the first package hitting targets around Sarajevo in the night time gloom. Ghost-like images of Hornets could be seen firing decoy flares as they delivered laser-guided bombs against targets in the hills around the Bosnian capital. Massive explosions reverberated around the city as Serb ammunition dumps took hits, along with SAM sites and command posts.

Sarajevo Strike Package Alpha involved 10 strike and four SEAD aircraft. UN artillery on Mount Igman now joined in the assault for just over an hour, firing some 600 rounds at Serb frontline artillery and tank positions. As dawn broke Sarajevo was shaken by the attacks of Strike Package Bravo going into action against more ammunition dumps. As the 14 strike and four SEAD aircraft had completed their work, a pair of reconnaissance aircraft swooped over the target area to assess the damage from the first three packages of the day.

Five hours later the 12 aircraft of Strike Package Charlie were sent to pound ammunition dumps and supply storage sites near the Bosnian Serb capital of Pale. A French Mirage 2000N K-2 of EC2/3 'Champagne' was hit by a SA-7 shoulder launched heat-seeking missile. The crew ejected and were captured in spite of several combat search and rescue operations mounted by US and French special forces helicopters. Two rescue missions came under Serb fire, and others were aborted due to bad weather. The Frenchmen were only freed in December after the signing of the Dayton Peace Accords.

NATO continued with its bombing campaign, with more ammuni-tion dumps being targeted by Strike Package Delta later in the afternoon. During the morning two Area SEAD packages of 12 and 25 aircraft respectively were launched to respond to any SAM threats. This exercise was repeated in the afternoon with two more Area SEAD packages of 19 and six aircraft on patrol. US Navy, US Marine and Spanish Hornets along with US Navy Prowlers flew these missions, but the Bosnian Serb Army air defensives remained 'hunkered down' and did not attempt to challenge NATO.

SARAJEVO CLOSE AIR SUPPORT

A close air support aircraft presence was maintained constantly over Sara-jevo throughout the day to protect UN troops. This involved 60 aircraft being cycled through a patrol pattern over the city between 4.30am and

Aircraft of several allied air forces flew as part of combined strike packages during Operation Allied Force. Here Dutch Lockheed Martin F-16A Fighting Falcons of 322nd Squadron and French *Armée de l'Air* Dassault Mirage 2000Ds of *3 Escadre de Chasse* are on a close air support patrol *(Tim Ripley)*

Royal Air Force BAe Harrier GR7s bore the brunt of the British offensive effort during Operation Deliberate Force with both laser-guided and conventional 'iron bombs' *(Jeremy Flack)*

midnight. During daylight, pairs of USAF A-10As and Dutch F-16s bore the brunt of this effort and on a number of occasions fired AGM-65 laser-guided Maverick missiles. Serb artillery, mortars, tanks, anti-aircraft missile teams and bunkers were all attacked after calls for help from UN tactical air control parties. When not responding to Serb fire, the close air support aircraft were directed at a number of fixed targets in the Sarajevo area. At night USAF Lockheed AC-130H Spectre gunships were called upon to attack and take out any misbehaving Serb gun positions. Some 10,000 rounds of 30mm, 40mm and 105mm ammunition were expended during nine actual close air support attacks around Sarajevo on 30 August 1995, the first day of Operation Deliberate Force.

Further reconnaissance missions to provide more photographs of bomb damage were flown at 6.30pm and 7.45pm by Dutch F-16s, US Navy TARPS equipped F-14s, French Mirage F1.CRs and British Harrier GR.7s. Strike Package Echo, made up of two strike aircraft and three SEAD aircraft hit another ammunition dump just after 7pm, to complete the first day's strike effort. Back at the Combined Air Operations Centre in Vicenza, Ryan's strike planning team were already at work preparing the air tasking message for the following day. By early evening aircraft were being prepared and crews briefed for the next day's five strike packages. These were again aimed at destroying Serb ammunition bunkers and supply depots around Sarajevo and Pale. Spectacular television images showed huge mushroom clouds around the city, followed by secondary explosions. These were plum targets that were ideal for destruction from the air by precision-guided munitions. UN artillery on Mount Igman continued to add to the bombardment, often being called at short notice to suppress Serb anti-aircraft missile teams that ventured into the open to take pot shots at NATO aircraft overhead.

BOMBING PAUSE

In the early hours of 1 September, NATO suspended its operations for 48 hours to give the Serbs time to withdraw their heavy weapons from around Sarajevo. Combined Air Operations Centre planners continued their work, sending close air support, fighter, reconnaissance, SEAD and surveillance missions over Bosnia. Strike packages were kept on ground alert at Italian bases, ready to go into action at a moment's notice, should a crisis develop. In spite of a few tanks being paraded in front of television cameras, NATO and the UN concluded that the Serbs had not complied with their demands to pull all heavy weapons out of the 20km exclusion zone by 11pm on 4 September. NATO strike aircraft were ordered back into action.

During 5 September four large strike packages hit a series of targets around Sarajevo, including the Lukovica barracks and a major storage ammunition complex at Hadizci. Huge explosions ripped through the targets indicating that the laser-guided bombs were striking full ammunition bunkers, not empty structures. The packages boasted around 20 aircraft each so it looked like a constant stream of bombs was raining down on Bosnian Serb Army positions around Sarajevo. Only the arrival of heavy cloud over the city in the afternoon spared the Serbs from yet more destruction.

Other strike aircraft ranged far over eastern Bosnia, including the Mount Jahorina bunker complex, communications sites near Tuzla, an ammunition dump at Visegrad and the Bosnian Serb Army alternative command bunker complex at Hans Pijesak. Bad weather, however, meant that many aircraft returned home with their bombs still on board. Some 50 SEAD aircraft supported the strike packages during the day.

Serb lines of communications next came under attack, with the Foca highway bridge being hit and badly damaged on 6 September. Bad weather hampered most NATO attacks during the day, but in the evening the weather cleared and NATO got back into its stride.

SEAD STRIKES

For the next five days, 5 ATAF continued to send five strike packages a day against targets in eastern Bosnia, mainly ammunition bunkers and bridges. In total some 12 bridges were attacked.

It was now becoming clear to NATO air commanders that their target list for eastern Bosnia was almost exhausted. Only a few days' worth of targets were left and Mladic had not agreed to UN and NATO demands to lift the siege of Sarajevo. Ryan and Admiral Smith decided to expand the target set to include air defence sites in north western Bosnia, around the city of Banja Luka. On 9 September the first of a series of what were called 'SEAD raids' were sent into action against Bosnian Serb Army air defence sites. A barrage of AGM-141 decoys was fired towards Banja Luka and a follow-up wave of some 33 HARMs was launched. Again the Serbs held their fire, although the USAF 23rd Fighter Squadron claimed the destruction of one SA-6 radar.

Plans were now being completed to employ Tomahawk Land Attack Missiles against the Lisna Mountain radar and communications hub to the north of Banja Luka during the evening of 10 September. General Janvier was given one more chance to meet Mladic and negotiate an end of the bombing.

Before the Tomahawk strike, French Jaguars and RAF Harriers carried out a decisive strike on a key telecommunications mast north of Tuzla, that connected Mladic's headquarters at Hans Pijesak with the key battle front to the west of Banja Luka. The British and French aircraft toppled the mast and knocked out a key Bosnian Serb Army communications link just as Croat troops were launching their offensive against Banja Luka. After the failure of Janvier's talks, 13 Tomahawk missiles were launched and a wave of US aircraft firing AGM-84 Stand-off Land Attack Missiles and GBU-15 optically-guided bombs hit Lisna and a number of other communications sites in western Bosnia. With their means of communications out of action, Bosnian Serb Army troops started to flee from the front, and Croat troops swept eastwards in a Blitzkrieg-style advance.

The momentum of the air offensive reached a new high the following day when 70 aircraft attacked targets in eastern Bosnia. By 12 September, the targets in the east were all but exhausted but a Bosnian Serb Army artillery attack on UN troops near Tuzla gave NATO the chance to start hitting a huge Serb ammunition dump at Doboj. Four massive packages were sent systematically to destroy the bunkers in the complex. One bomb detonated several tons of artillery shells, creating a huge mushroom cloud and shattering windows in down-town Doboj several miles away, leading the Serbs to accuse NATO of using tactical nuclear weapons.

Four strike packages were planned for 13 September but bad weather grounded 40% of the aircraft. The last bombs of the campaign were dropped late in the afternoon on a tank repair yard and ammunition dump near Sarajevo.

The Lisna communications mast complex and radar site was hit by Tomahawk Land Attack Missiles fired from the USS *Normandy* on 10th September, disrupting Serb communications in western Bosnia just as the Croat ground offensive was gathering momentum. This is the post-strike imagery from a General Atomics Predator UAV *(US DoD/JCC(D))*

ENTER HOLBROOKE

With NATO bombers running out of targets, the US peace envoy Richard Holbrooke was ordered to Belgrade to see if Milosevic could persuade Mladic to lift the siege of Sarajevo. The rapid Croat advances on the back of NATO's air strikes around Banja Luka, Tuzla and Doboj, had at last convinced Mladic that he had to do a deal. Milosevic had threatened to abandon the Bosnian Serb Army to its fate unless he signed up to pulling back his guns from Sarajevo. With little option, Mladic agreed to a ceasefire around Sarajevo, to pull his heavy guns back, and to open the airport and road routes into the city for humanitarian aid. In return, NATO would stop bombing, allowing Mladic to concentrate on fighting the Croats and Bosnians in the north west.

As news emerged of the deal during 14 September, 5 ATAF reverted to a ground alert posture for its strike aircraft. An intense air presence was maintained over Bosnia to search out fresh targets and to be ready to provide close air support for UN troops on the ground.

The Serbs were given until 10pm on 16 September to withdraw all their heavy weapons from the Sarajevo 20 kilometer exclusion zone. This was later extended by 72 hours as many of the Serb tanks were broken down and there was a shortage of fuel for artillery tow trucks. NATO reconnaissance aircraft and Predator UAVs were very active verifying that this was a real withdrawal not another Serb propaganda stunt.

COLOUR PLATES

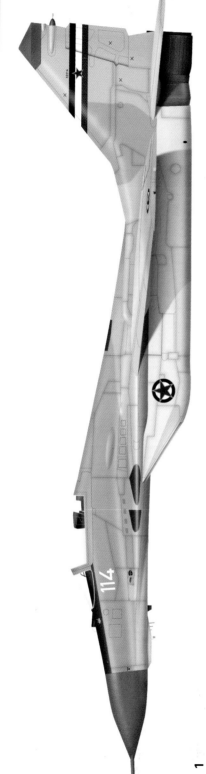

1
Mikoyan MiG-29, Serial Number: 18114, 127th 'Knights' Fighter Squadron, Jugoslaensko Ratno Vazduhoplovsto (JRV) (Yugoslav Air Force), Batajnica Airbase, Belgrade, Serbia, July 1991

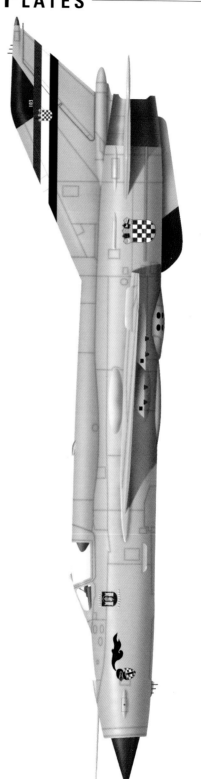

2
Mikoyan Gurevich MiG-21bis, Serial Number: 103, 1st Fighter Squadron, Hrvatsko Ratno Zrakoplvstvo (HRZ)(Croatian War Aviation), Pleso Airport, Zagreb, Croatia, June 1992

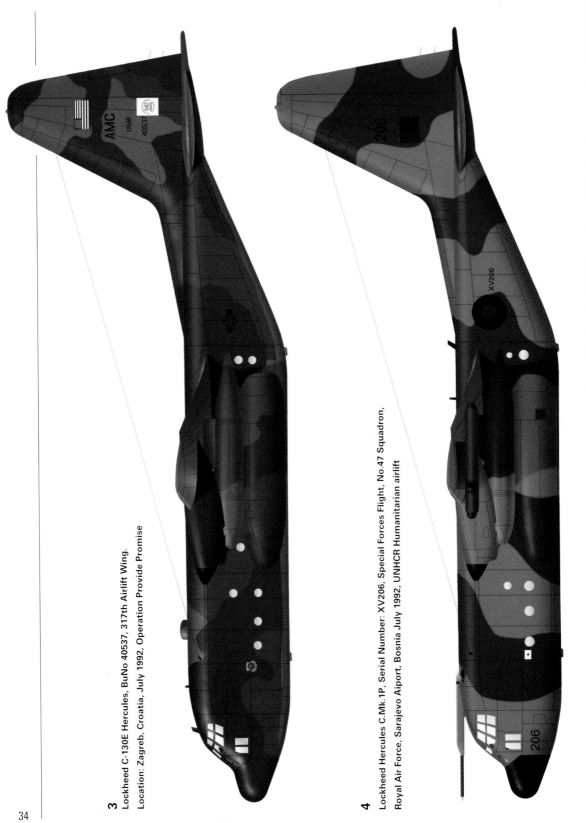

3

Lockheed C-130E Hercules, BuNo 40537, 317th Airlift Wing.

Location: Zagreb, Croatia, July 1992, Operation Provide Promise

4

Lockheed Hercules C.Mk.1P, Serial Number: XV206, Special Forces Flight, No.47 Squadron, Royal Air Force, Sarajevo Aiport, Bosnia July 1992, UNHCR Humanitarian airlift

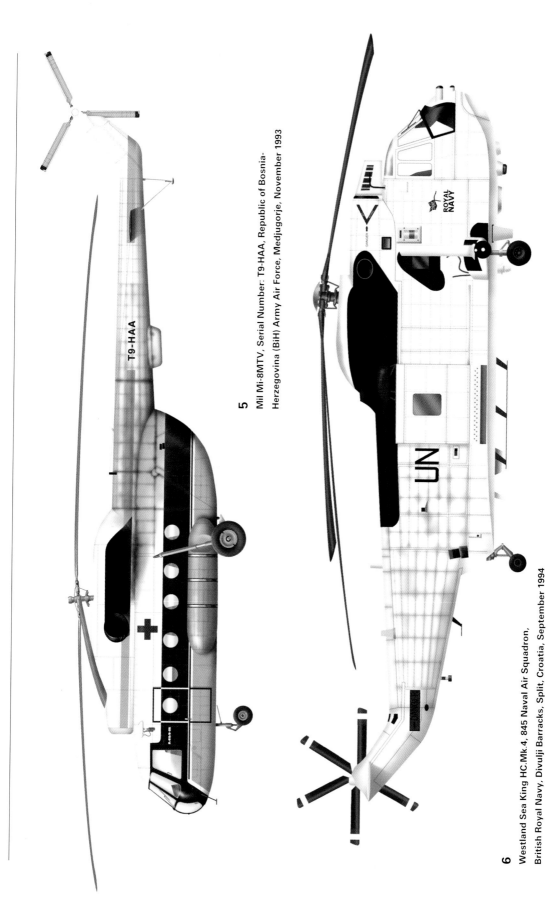

5

Mil Mi-8MTV, Serial Number: T9-HAA, Republic of Bosnia-Herzegovina (BiH) Army Air Force, Medjugorje, November 1993

6

Westland Sea King HC.Mk.4, 845 Naval Air Squadron, British Royal Navy, Divulji Barracks, Split, Croatia, September 1994

7

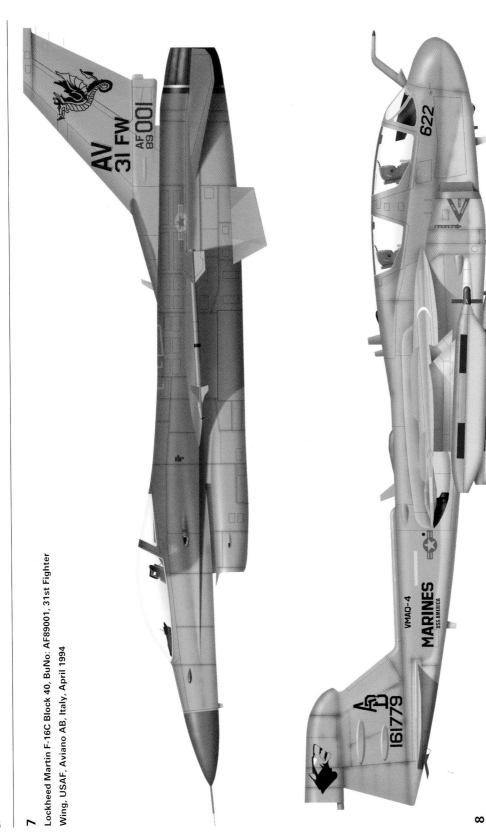

Lockheed Martin F-16C Block 40, BuNo: AF89001, 31st Fighter
Wing, USAF, Aviano AB, Italy, April 1994

8

Grumman EA-6B Prowler, BuNo 161779, Marine Tactical Electronic
Warfare Squadron 4 (VMAQ-4), USMC, USS *America*, Operation
Deliberate Force, September 1995

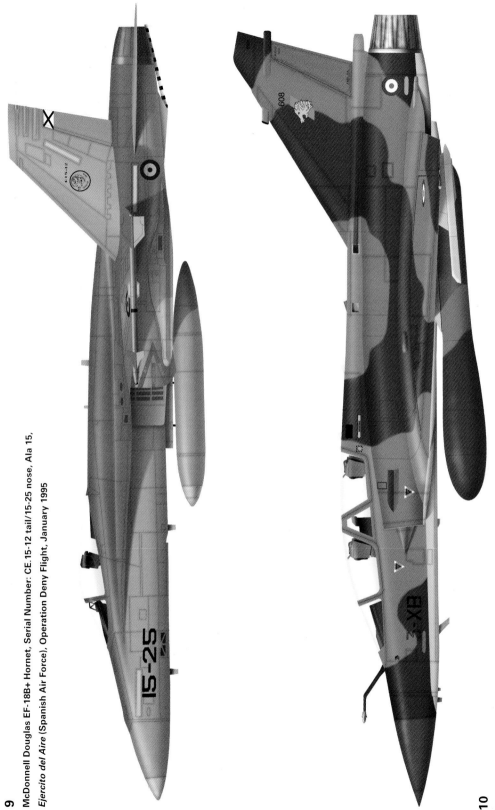

9

McDonnell Douglas EF-18B+ Hornet, Serial Number: CE.15-12 tail/15-25 nose, Ala 15, *Ejercito del Aire* (Spanish Air Force), Operation Deny Flight, January 1995

10

Dassault Mirage 2000D, Serial Number: 3-XB, 3e *Escadron de Chasse* 'Ardennes', of 3e *Escadre de Chasse*, (EC3/3), Operation Deliberate Force, September 1995

11

McDonnell Douglas F/A-18C Hornet, BuNo 164632, Strike Fighter Squadron 87 (VFA-87)/Carrier Air Wing 8 (CVW-8), USS Theodore Roosevelt, Operation Allied Force, May 1999

12

British Aerospace Harrier GR.Mk.7, Serial Number: ZD437, No 1 (Fighter) Squadron, Royal Air Force, Gioia del Colle AB, Italy, Operation Allied Force, May 1999

13

Fairchild A-10A Warthog, BuNo 80654, 91st Fighter Squadron, USAF, Gioia del

Colle AB, Italy, May 1999, Operation Allied Force

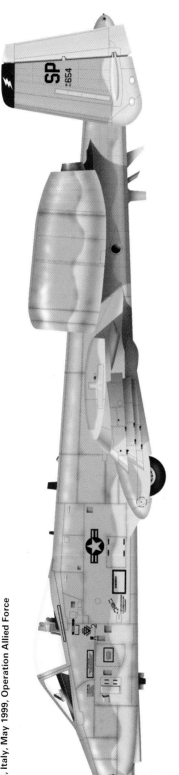

14

Boeing Chinook HC.Mk.2, No. 27 Squadron, Royal Air Force, Camp Piper,

Macedonia, 11th June 1999

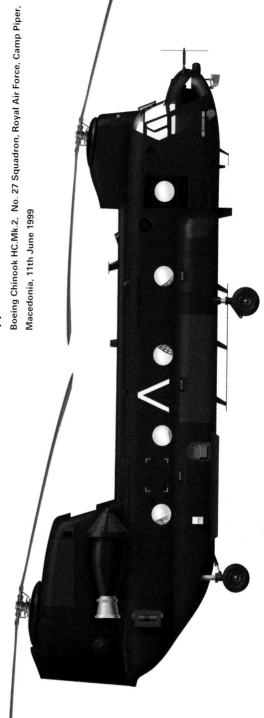

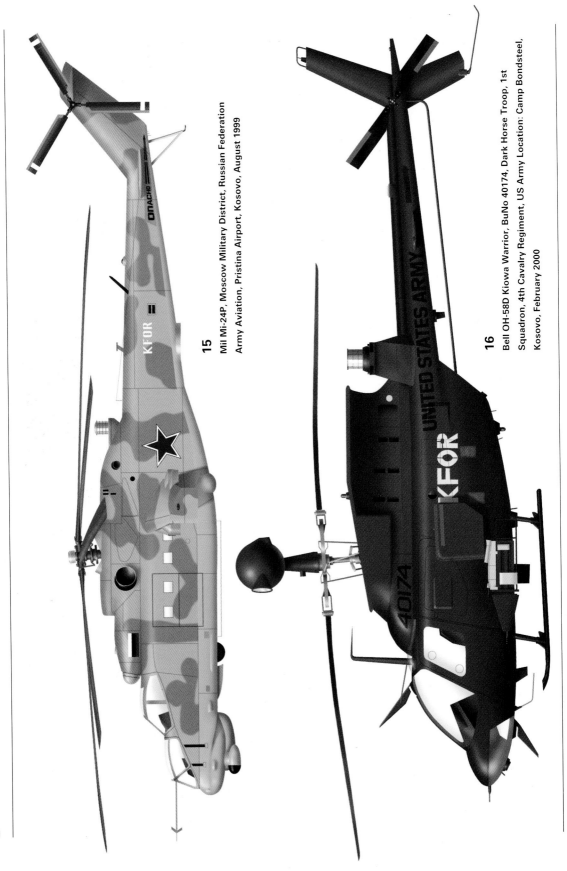

15

Mil Mi-24P, Moscow Military District, Russian Federation
Army Aviation, Pristina Airport, Kosovo, August 1999

16

Bell OH-58D Kiowa Warrior, BuNo 40174, Dark Horse Troop, 1st
Squadron, 4th Cavalry Regiment, US Army Location: Camp Bondsteel,
Kosovo, February 2000

1

2

3

41

4

5

6

7

8

9

10

A race now began to get the UNHCR airbridge operating again. It had been closed since April because of continuous heavy fighting around the airport. The honour of making the first landing at Sarajevo airport fell to an *Armée de l'Air* C-130 on 15 September, which brought in the French defence minister on a morale boosting visit to the predominately French UN garrison that had been largely cut off since May. The next day the airbridge got into full swing when eight aircraft landed at Sarajevo's battered airport. Ancona in Italy was now the main hub for the UNHCR effort, with British, Canadian and USAF C-130s joining their French colleagues, along with German C.160Ds. The UNHCR aimed to have eight to 10 flights a day flying into the city. White painted UN Protection Force Il-76s also started using the airport to bring in much needed supplies for the UN garrison. Within a few days road convoys had free access to the city, reducing the need for the airbridge but the UNHCR kept it going for three more months to empty its large warehouses at Ancona and Split.

The re-opening of Sarajevo airport was the first tangible sign that Operation Deliberate Force had had some effect on the behaviour of the Bosnian Serb Army. During the operation some 3,515 sorties were flown by aircraft from nine allied air forces. These included 750 strike sorties against some 56 fixed targets, which inflicted heavy damage against 81% of those hit.

On 20 September, Admiral Smith and General Janvier flew into Sarajevo to assess Serb compliance with the UN and NATO ultimatum. With the Serbs having pulled back some 250 tanks and heavy weapons the two commanders were able to declare Operation Deliberate Force a success. NATO's airpower was stood down.

The operation, however, did not end the war. Bosnian Serb Army troops were mounting a fierce defence of Banja Luka, and Holbrooke had still successfully to conclude his peace mission. In this tense and confused situation, NATO aircraft continued to patrol over Bosnia. On 4 October US Marine Corps Prowlers reported being illuminated by Serb missile guidance radars and fired three HARM missiles in response.

NATO's final strike mission of the war was flown on 9 October 1995 in response to a Bosnian Serb artillery attack on the UN base at Tuzla. Working with a Danish tactical air control party on the ground, an Airborne Forward Air Control F-16 of the USAF 510th Fighter Squadron found the offending Serb artillery battery near Mount Zep. The 'Buzzard' fired a Mk 66 white phosphorous or 'Willie Pete' at the target but missed. The tactical air control party radioed corrections and the F-16 successfully marked the target. Five other F-16s then demolished the target with laser-guided bombs, to complete the first ever F-16 Airborne Forward Air Control mission.

Bell 206 Jet Rangers on charter to the UN Peace Forces in Croatia were in heavy demand during 1995 to fly international peace envoys around the former Yugoslavia *(Tim Ripley)*

END GAME

Holbrooke finished his negotiations in early October and on 20 October a cease fire at last took hold along Bosnia's frontlines. Barely a month later Serb, Croat and Bosnian political leaders at last signed up to the Dayton Peace Accords, ending the war and opening the way for NATO to deploy its peace Implementation Force (IFOR) to take over from the UN Protection Force on 20 December 1996. 5 ATAF simply chopped command to become IFOR's air component. Its aircraft continued to police the skies over Bosnia looking for prohibited military air activity; they flew close air support for IFOR troops being threatened by former warring faction troops and conducted extensive air reconnaissance to look for activity breaching the Dayton accords. IFOR troops and NATO aircraft were mandated vigorously to enforce the military provisions of the Dayton accords.

Deploying IFOR's 60,000 troops rapidly to prevent a security vacuum developing meant a major airlift effort was needed. While British, French and other allied countries simply transferred control of their troops in Bosnia from UN to IFOR command, there were no US forces in the Balkans. The first US troops arrived ahead of the transfer of authority from the UN to prepare Tuzla Airbase to be the main operating base of Task Force Falcon.

C-130 aircraft flew through terrible December weather to

USAF/US Army Northrop Grumman E-8 Joint-STARS airborne ground surveillance aircraft were dispatched to Rhein-Main AB, Germany, in December 1995, to support the move of NATO forces into Bosnia *(US DoD/JCC(D))*

German forces played a major role in both the IFOR and SFOR missions, including the provision of VFW-Fokker CH-53G Sea Stallion heavy lift helicopters from *Heersfliegerregiment I (Victor Kuhn/HFR 15)*

The USAF deployed a huge airlift element to Rhein-Main AB in Germany, including McDonnell Douglas C-17 Globemasters, Lockheed C-141Starlifters and C-5 Galaxys, to support the movement of the US Army contingent to Bosnia in December 1995 and January 1996 *(Tim Ripley)*

deliver a US Army airborne task force to Tuzla to secure it until the main body of the 1st Armoured Division could drive down through Croatia from its forward base at Taszar in Hungary.

Winter storms prevented US Army engineers bridging the River Sava on the Croatia-Bosnia border in the final days of December 1995, so the USAF's Air Mobility Command was called upon to set up an airbridge to start flying tanks, helicopters and other heavy equipment to reinforce the paratroopers at Tuzla.

The 1st Armoured Division's Aviation Brigade was pushed forward to protect the bridging site at the River Sava with its McDonnell Douglas AH-64A Apache attack helicopters. Elements of the brigade pushed deep into Bosnia, setting up an advanced base at Tuzla ahead of the division's main body. The brigade's Apache unit, the 2nd Battalion, 227th Aviation Regiment, was deployed throughout Bosnia supporting allied as well as US forces. They were prominent in Sarajevo flying security patrols during the visits of senior NATO commanders and international diplomats. US Army Sikorsky UH-60 Blackhawks also moved French special forces to raid a radical Muslim Mujahideen guerrilla base near Sarajevo.

British forces also made heavy use of helicopters during their move into north west Bosnia to establish a buffer line between Serb and Croat/ Muslim forces. RAF Boeing Chinook HC.2 and Royal Navy Sea Kings were used to fly Royal Artillery gun batteries to fire positions to cover British columns as they pushed northwards to establish a zone of separation between Serb, Croat and Muslim forces. The British also established an aviation battlegroup based around 9 Regiment Army Air Corps. Its TOW missile armed Lynx AH.7 anti-tank helicopters provided welcome overhead protection to British troops in several tense incidents, including

General Atomics Predator UAV bases at Taszar in Hungary have flown regular surveillance missions over the Balkans since the start of the IFOR mission *(General Atomics)*

47

The immense fire power of the McDonnell Douglas AH-64A Apache attack helicopters serving with IFOR and SFOR has played a major part in ensuring the former warring factions do not breach the military terms of the Dayton Peace Accords *(US DoD/JCC(D))*

one in which a column of Muslim troops and tanks tried to occupy a Croat controlled area. The presence of British troops and helicopters defused the situation.

By the summer of 1996 Bosnia was largely quiet and NATO forces began re-orientating themselves to providing support to the rebuilding of the war ravaged country. Heavy lift helicopters helped repair bridges and buildings. Other helicopters evacuated wounded civilians and moved mine clearing teams into place. As a demonstration of NATO's resolve to keep the peace, IFOR established a field firing range at Glamoc in western Bosnia, where US Army Apaches and British Lynxes regularly test fired their weaponry.

In December 1996, IFOR handed over to the new NATO military force, dubbed the Stabilisation Force (SFOR), but 5 ATAF continued going about its business in much the same way as before. NATO fighter and strike aircraft from America, Canada, Belgium, Britain, France, Germany, Holland, Italy, Spain and Turkey continued to make daily sweeps over Bosnia to support Alliance ground troops. There was a minor crisis during the run up to the September 1997 elections, which saw the US Army's Apaches in heavy demand to provide air cover for isolated NATO ground units. The crisis passed and since then Bosnia has largely been peaceful.

The American commanders of IFOR, and then SFOR, have had a flight of Sikorky UH-60 Blackhawk helicopters at their disposal to fly them anywhere in the Balkans *(NATO)*

French and German Bombardier CL-289 umanned reconnaissance drones were sent to Bosnia in 1996 to monitor compliance with the military terms of the Dayton Peace Accords *(Dornier)*

ALBANIA RESCUE

A new area of operations for NATO opened in Albania in March 1997 when the country collapsed into chaos as a result of a financial crisis. Rioting broke out in the capital and American and European nationals were ordered to leave the country. SFOR in Bosnia was tasked with organising the evacuation operation with its helicopters, while 5 ATAF was available to provide aircover. Operation Silver Wake began with Cobra, Sea Stallion and Sikorsky CH-46 Sea Knight helicopters making a daylight mission from a USS amphibious warfare vessel in the Adriatic. When a Cobra commander spotted someone armed with a SA-7 missile near the pick-up point, he engaged the man with the helicopter's 20mm cannon. British Chinooks flew in a contingent of SAS troops to guard the landing zone, while German Army CH-53Gs took part as well. The *Heersflieger* crews gained the distinction of being the first German soldiers since World War Two to fire shots in anger when helicopter door gunners fired back after the evacuation helicopters started taking fire.

As the evacuation operation was underway, air protection packages of F-16s, Hornets and Prowlers were launched from Aviano Airbase, Italy, to make sure the helicopters made it safely to ships offshore or bases in Italy during the four day long evacuation operation. In the end the fighter protection was unnecessary, but the aircraft did become involved in escorting Albanian MiG-17 fighters defecting to Italy.

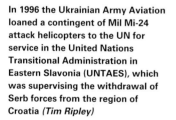

In 1996 the Ukrainian Army Aviation loaned a contingent of Mil Mi-24 attack helicopters to the UN for service in the United Nations Transitional Administration in Eastern Slavonia (UNTAES), which was supervising the withdrawal of Serb forces from the region of Croatia *(Tim Ripley)*

PART 2: CRISIS OVER KOSOVO 1998 – 2000

CIVIL WAR

The disputed province of Kosovo had been a festering hot bed of tension between the ethnic Albanian majority and its Serb rulers for a decade. The violent break up of the old Socialist Federal Republic of Yugoslavia in the early 1990s largely passed Kosovo by, with the 1.8 million ethnic Albanians adopting passive resistance tactics in their bid for independence. A series of violent clashes between Serb para-military security forces and a shadowy group known as the Kosovo Liberation Army (KLA or UCK) in the spring of 1998 steadily escalated during the year, until the province was in the grip of all out war. Diplomatic intervention by the US Balkan trouble shooter Dick Holbrooke in October 1998 calmed the situation and paved the way for the deployment of the ceasefire monitoring teams of the Kosovo Verification Mission, (KVM) protected by NATO's Extraction Force based in neighbouring Macedonia. The battalion sized British, French, Dutch, German and Italian force was backed up by an aviation element containing Dutch Boeing CH-47D Chinooks, Italian Agusta A-129 Mangustas and AB212s, and French Aerospatiale SA.330 Pumas and Gazelles.

This ceasefire never really took hold and in the Spring of 1999 western diplomats tried to broker an end to the war at two negotiating sessions in France. By late March, the peace talks had failed and NATO air forces were ordered into action. It was hoped that the Serb leadership would buckle under the pressure and sign up to the peace plan.

In parallel with the build-up of diplomatic pressure the NATO allies began reinforcing their air assets in range of the Balkans, ready to strike at Yugoslavia. The first wave of reinforcements arrived in February 1999, with eight cruise missile armed USAF Boeing B-52 Stratofortress bombers arriving at RAF Fairford in the United Kingdom. A dozen

Dutch Air Force Boeing CH-47D Chinook helicopters deployed to Macedonia in January 1999 to support the NATO Extraction Force (NATO EF PIO)

Boeing B-52 Stratofortresses from the 11th, 20th, 23rd and 96th Bomb Squadrons deployed to RAF Fairford in Britain to form the 2nd Expeditionary Operations Group *(US DoD/JCC(D))*

Lockheed F-117A Night Hawk stealth fighters were sent to Aviano Airbase in Italy, along with a contingent of Grumman EA-6B Prowlers. Some 29 tankers, 25 Boeing KC-135 Stratotankers and four McDonnell Douglas KC-10A Extenders, were forward deployed at a number of bases, including Sigonella Naval Air Station on Sicily, Moron Airbase in Spain and RAF Mildenhall in the UK. These were in addition to tankers already deployed in Europe at Mildenhall, Istres in France and Aviano, under the control of the 100th Air Refueling Wing.

The armada of some 250 allied aircraft, including 200 from the USAF, was placed under the operational control of the Combined Air Operation Centre at Dal Molin Airbase, near Vicenza, Italy. NATO's southern European air commander, USAF Lieutenant General Mike Short, masterminded the build-up of forces from his headquarters in Naples. As the time to launch the strikes approached, General Short flew up to Vicenza to run the war from the hi-tech Combined Air Operations Centre housed in a prefabricated building alongside Dal Molin's runway. It boasted computer and satellite links to all NATO airbases taking part in the operation and near-real time data links to key surveillance assets monitoring the Balkans, such as the Lockheed U-2R Dragon Lady reconnaissance aircraft, Boeing E-3A Sentry AWACS radar surveillance aircraft and US reconnaissance satellites. The staff used computer systems to develop and transmit the daily air tasking message. This contained all the operational, targetting, communications, routing and other data needed to allow allied pilots to co-ordinate their missions. No allied aircraft flew over the Balkans, except for USAF stealth aircraft, without being included in the NATO air tasking message, to ensure every aircraft was working to common radio frequencies and all flight plans were co-ordinated. The Combined Air Operation Centre was set up in 1993 to control the no-fly zone over Bosnia and it has been in continuous operation since then. This allowed it almost seamlessly to extend its area of operations to cover Kosovo during late 1998 when Operation Eagle Eye was launched. Close co-operation was developed with the KVM monitors on the ground in Kosovo, via the NATO Kosovo Verification Co-ordination Centre (KVCC) in Kumonavo, Macedonia. The KVCC intelligence cell worked closely with the KVM to identify and locate all Serb forces inside Kosovo. This information was to prove invaluable to the target planning teams in the Combined Air Operations Centre.

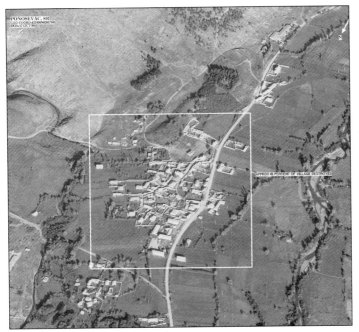

PONOSEVAC, SIR
GEO COORD:42N08N0N0517051
DOB:17 OCT 1991

APPROX 45 PERCENT OF VILLAGE DESTROYED

Lockheed U-2S Dragon Lady reconnaissance aircraft provided detailed evidence of the conflict in Kosovo during Operations Eagle Eye and Allied Force (AFSOUTH)

When the KVM monitors were withdrawn from Kosovo on 20 March 1999, the KVCC intelligence analysts were absorbed into the NATO Allied Command Europe Rapid Reaction Corps (ARRC) Headquarters which had just arrived in Macedonia to command western ground troops in the small Balkan country.

FIRST STRIKE

After the breakdown of peace talks in Paris during the third week of March, NATO's political leaders authorised what became known as Operation Allied Force. This was intended to be a three phase campaign with limited objectives. Phase one was to be the degradation of the Yugoslav integrated air defence systems. Phase two was progressively to degrade Yugoslav army (VJ) and para-military Ministry of Interior special police units, through attacks on logistics facilities, supply routes and finally troops in the field. Crucially phase two was limited to targets below the 44th Parallel, forming what became known as the 'Kosovo theatre of operations'. The final phase of the operation was to spread the campaign to attack phase two target sets throughout Yugoslavia. The plan was sequential in nature, with senior NATO political leaders and military planners not envisaging phase two and three being executed until the Yugoslav air defences had been pummelled for a long time. NATO's supreme political body, the North Atlantic Council demanded that it authorise the move to different phases of the campaign and only the forces required to execute phase one were deployed at the start of the operation. Political leaders in Washington and other allied capitals were convinced that Milosevic would give in after a few days of bombing. They only authorised a list of 50 targets, and demanded that the loss of life among Yugoslav military and police personnel was minimal. For example, only empty barracks and remote communications or radar sites could be attacked. This was to be a classic case of using military power to send political signals. Some western military men compared the operation to the strategy employed during the Vietnam war. The result was disastrous for the people of Kosovo.

WEATHERED OUT

Operation Allied Force got underway at 8.00pm local time on the evening of 24th March, with a salvo of scores of air and sea launched cruise missiles fired from USAF B-52s, US Navy ships and a Royal Navy submarine in the Adriatic. Some 23 air defence sites throughout Yugoslavia were hit and three waves of manned aircraft were then launched against more air defence sites, as well as airfields, command posts and communication sites.

McDonnell Douglas F-15E Strike Eagle bombers used a wide variety of laser and optically-guided munitions to destroy hundreds of targets with great precision (US DoD/JCC(D))

The Yugoslav air force's main operating base at Batajnica, near Belgrade, was heavily targeted by NATO but all of Serbia's frontline fighters had long been moved to dispersed field locations (US DoD/JCC(D))

Yugoslav defences had been on full alert for several days after the break down of the peace talks, with key assets such as fighter aircraft, surface-to-air missile (SAM) launchers, artillery and armoured vehicles being moved out of their bases into the countryside. The live broadcasts on CNN of the take off of the B-52s from their base Britain during the morning of the 24th gave the Yugoslav air defence command in Zenum even more precise warning that the allied attack was underway.

Multi-national packages of aircraft flew these missions, with bomb droppers supported by fighter combat air patrols, suppression of enemy air defence aircraft (SEAD), AWACS radar surveillance aircraft, air refuelling tankers, electronic intelligence gathering aircraft and backed up by combat search and rescue helicopters.

The first cruise missile strikes damaged but did not put the Yugoslav air defences out of action, so when the manned NATO aircraft approached enemy territory four MiG-29 fighters were scrambled to intercept them. As a NATO strike package approached the Yugoslav capital Belgrade, Dutch F-16s and USAF F-15Cs were vectored to intercept by a NATO E-3A AWACS. A RAF BAe Nimrod R1 electronic surveillance aircraft positively identified the MiG-29s as hostile, clearing the NATO fighters to engage the Yugoslav aircraft. Three of the MiGs were downed by NATO AMRAAM missiles, with one kill being claimed by the Royal Netherlands Air Force's 322nd Squadron.

By dawn all the allied aircraft had returned to their bases, with many of the pilots reporting the experience as one of the most demanding of their careers. The air-to-air refuelling phase of the raid was particularly challenging because many pilots were refuelling in the dark from unfamiliar types of tankers. Only by luck were mid-air collisions avoided in some cases. Serb air defences were also very active and made NATO suppression of enemy air defense forces work hard. It was with great relief to many of the allied pilots when they turned for home.

Satellites and U-2 reconnaissance aircraft now did their work to provide the battle damage assessment cell in the Combined Air

BATAJNICA AIR FORCE REPAIR BASE, SERBIA

Operations Centre with a crucial up-date on the progress of the first wave of air attacks. This procedure became almost routine as the allied aircraft returned to the skies over Yugoslavia.

The strength of the Serb air defence network meant NATO limited itself to night time only strikes in the first few days of Operation Allied Force. During daylight hours NATO's air forces were still in the skies, providing a constant stream of aircraft to fill combat air patrol stations over countries threatened by the Yugoslav air forces, including Albania, Bosnia, Hungary and Macedonia. A constant protective presence also had to be maintained over the Adriatic to deter Yugoslav attacks on the NATO fleet patrolling off Montenegro.

The value of these patrols was demonstrated when a pair of F-15Cs over Bosnia was vectored to intercept two MiG-29s flying towards the country. They were soon intercepted and crashed after being hit by the Americans' missiles, to the north east of Tuzla. The two pilots ejected, but were recovered by Russian troops serving with the NATO Stabilisation Force (SFOR) in Bosnia and delivered back to safety in Yugoslavia.

This was not the only incursion into Bosnian airspace, with a flight of Serb Mil Mi-8 HIP helicopters being detected by an AWACS on 26 March. Again USAF F-15Cs were vectored to intercept, but after they illuminated the two helicopters with their radar, the intruders dropped down into a valley and made a rapid escape back into Yugoslavia. Bosnian airspace played a crucial role in the conflict, allowing allied aircraft and cruise missiles easy access to key targets within

Jubilant Yugoslav troops examine the wreckage of the USAF Lockheed F-117 Nighthawk stealth fighter on 27th March 1999

Yugoslavia. NATO immediately closed the country's airspace to civilian traffic to allow it unimpeded access. Sarajevo, Mostar and Banja Luka airports were closed to civilian flights, and Sarajevo was nominated as a military diversion airport. At least two NATO jets made use of the airport, one F-15C reportedly landed there trailing white smoke after accidentally taking a hit from 20mm cannon fire from his wing man during a combat air patrol.

NATO remained on high alert for surprise Serb air attacks throughout this time with upwards of one quarter to a third of all allied air sorties being devoted to air defence. The British also asked the USAF to loan them a Lockheed C-5 Galaxy to fly out a battery of Shorts High Velocity Missiles to protect Petrovec airport in Macedonia on 28 March.

The manned element of the NATO strike force was initially dependent on Paveway series laser-guided bombs and other precision-guided munitions which relied on optical guidance. Tight rules of engagement were instituted to prevent collateral damage to the civilian population but bad weather meant that allied pilots had great difficulty meeting the requirements laid down to allow weapon release. Thick cloud belts and heavy rain meant pilots could not find their targets or maintain good laser locks. During the first eight days of the war more than half the NATO strike sorties were aborted. On several days during the early part of the conflict no bombs could be dropped and NATO had to rely only on its cruise missiles to hit its target sets.

The air offensive suffered a major setback on the night of 27/28 March when an F-117 was lost near the Yugoslavian capital Belgrade in mysterious circumstances. Jubilant Yugoslav military commanders claimed to have shot the stealth fighter down with a surface-to-air-missile but the USAF has so far refused to say how the $40 million plane was lost. Video footage of the wreckage showed what appeared to be 30mm cannon holes in the wings, perhaps indicating that the so-called radar 'invisible' aircraft fell victim to anti-aircraft fire or even a MiG. The only redeeming feature of the incident was an efficient combat search and rescue mounted by USAF Special Operations Command. Sikorsky MH-53J Pave Low III helicopters scrambled from Tuzla Airbase in Bosnia. USAF Fairchild A-10A Warthogs flew 'Sandy' cover for the mission which successfully plucked the pilot to safety from deep inside Yugoslavia. The rescue force took several hours to find the downed pilot, with USAF KC-135R and Lockheed MC-130 Combat Talon tankers refuelling the MH-53Js and A-10As during the operation.

Within days another aerial search operation would have to be launched after three US Army soldiers serving in Macedonia were ambushed and captured by a Serb special forces team. When the soldiers radioed in that they were under attack, the air operations centre in the Shoe Factory headquarters of the ARRC(Allied Command Europe Rapid Reaction Corps) in Skopje, co-ordinated an air search involving British Army Air Corps Lynx AH.7s of 659 Squadron, and French Army Aviation Gazelles. A USAF Special Operations Command Lockheed AC-130 Spectre gunship joined the effort with its powerful night observation equipment, but by the early morning on 31 March the search was called off after the three hapless GIs were paraded on Belgrade television.

HELPING THE REFUGEES

Within days of the NATO air campaign being launched the Yugoslav regime decided to step up its counter-insurgency effort against the KLA/UCK by beginning a massive programme of 'ethnic cleansing' to expel all of Kosovo's ethnic Albanian population. Hundreds of thousands of people fled over the borders into Albania and Macedonia and overwhelmed the resources of the on-the-scene humanitarian agencies. NATO's strategy of sending a political signal to Belgrade had failed. Milosevic was fighting back. Western leaders were thrown into disarray. Pronouncements by US President Bill Clinton and British Prime Minister Tony Blair that ground troops would not be used had only served to encourage Milosevic. There was little idea what to do next, apart from to continue the bombing. Until the Washington summit in mid April, NATO military commanders had little formal guidance as to the alliance's aims and objectives.

On the ground in the Balkans, NATO military forces were ordered to go to the aid of the refugees, establishing camps in Macedonia and airlifting aid into Albania, Greece and Macedonia. Petrovec airport in Macedonia became the focus for an international airlift of aid from more than a dozen countries. Some 30 flights, mainly by military C-130s, a day were landing at the airport to be unloaded by NATO troops. British, French, Dutch and Italian helicopters based at Petrovec airport swung into action carrying relief, supplied to the scores of refugee camps that sprang up in Macedonia during April to accommodate the hundreds of thousands of refugees pouring over the border.

USAF Tactical Airlift Control Elements deployed to both Petrovec in Macedonia and Thesseloniki in Greece to off-load out sized cargoes from USAF Boeing C-17s, Lockheed C-5s, C-130s, and C-141s. The aircraft were based in Europe at Ramstein in Germany and Ancona in Italy for Operation Shining Hope, as the US portion of the aid operation was code-named. At these bases the aid from continental US stores would be unloaded from commercial Boeing 747s, before being stowed on the military transports for the flights to the heart of the Balkans.

The mountainous terrain in Albania proved to be a greater challenge for international military forces sent to help the refugees. First on the scene were elements of the

Civilian flights continued to operate from Macedonia's Petrovec Airport throughout the conflict, making it one of the busiest airports in the world as scores of aid aircraft competed with civilian traffic *(Land Command/Media Operations)*

USAF McDonnell Douglas C-17 Globemaster transports made hundreds of sorties into the short runway at Rinas airport to deploy the men and equipment of Task Force Hawk *(US DoD/JCC(D))*

Sikorsky MH-53E Sea Dragon helicopters flying off the USS *Inchon* were put to good use flying aid to refugee camps throughout Albania *(US DoD/JCC(D))*

US Marines embark on a Sikorsky CH-53E Sea Stallion of the 26th Marine Expeditionary Unit – Special Operations Capable in the build up to the NATO move into Kosovo *(US DoD/JCC(D))*

Italian Navy and San Marco marine battalion, who are based just across the Adriatic at Brindisi. Italian Navy HH-3F of *32 Stormo* made the first flights up to border regions near Kukes with supplies for the refugees. USAF Special Operations Command Sikorsky MH-53Js of the US Joint Special Operations Task Force at Brindisi soon joined this effort, alongside US Navy Sikorsky CH-53Es of HC-4 flying from their forward logistic support site (FLSS) base at Bari. But the Americans only flew to Kukes for one day because the Serb surface-to-air missile threat was considered to be too high. The US helicopters then concentrated on supplying refugee camps along the border and US Marine Corps CH-53Es also joined this mission, flying off the amphibious assault ships *Inchon*, *Nassau* and *Kearsage* which were cruising in the Adriatic.

The UNHCR call for help to supply the thousands of refugees gathered in terrible condition at

Kukes was soon answered by French, Swiss and United Arab Emirates Pumas, Austrian Bell 412s, Greek and Dutch Chinooks, Ukrainian Mil Mi-8s and a number of chartered civilian helicopters.

A USAF Tactical Airlift Control Element took over responsibility for air traffic control at Tirana's Rinas airport, which soon grew to be one of the busiest heliports in Europe handling more than 200 movements a day. Actual tasking of flights was carried out by UNHCR and RAF Support Helicopter Force Headquarters experts from their ad hoc command post at Rinas airport.

The airport became the main entry point for air delivered aid, with flights from the US, UK, Belgium, France, Saudi Arabia and other nations regularly bringing in supplies. At the end of April, NATO's Albania Force headquarters had been established at the port of Durres to co-ordinate the relief effort. It only had a tenuous control on the multi-national forces arriving in the country, and no authority over the American combat forces that were soon to mass at Rinas airport.

Elements of the Royal Air Force's Support Helicopter Force Headquarters deployed to Rinas airport in Albania to co-ordinate the UNHCR humanitarian effort to move aid by helicopter to border refugee camps (HQ SHF)

McDonnell Douglas AH-64A Apache helicopters, of 6th Squadron, 6th Cavalry Regiment, were one of two attack helicopter battalions assigned to Task Force Hawk. The unit later moved to Macedonia to support the NATO land invasion of Kosovo in June 1999 (US DoD/JCC(D))

APACHE FORCE

In another bid to increase the kill rate of Serb armour and heavy equipment, the Pentagon decided to send a brigade of AH-64A Apache attack helicopters to Albania, The Pentagon said its so-called Task Force Hawk was to get 'up close and personal' with the Serbs. From the beginning the deployment of the attack helicopters was to be dogged by bad luck.

Initially Rinas airport was clogged with aid flights, preventing the start of a shuttle of C-17s from Germany with the task force's logistic support equipment. It was not until the third week of April that the first

Apaches would fly into Rinas after self deploying to Brindisi in southern Italy. The anarchic nature of Albania and the long reach of Serb multiple rocket launchers also made the US government cautious about allowing its troops to go anywhere near the crucial border region with Kosovo. The crash of an AH-64 three days after their arrival at Rinas, following a tree strike, did not help the task force's image. Another crash cost the lives of two Apache air crew.

Rinas airport in Albania was turned into a major NATO logistic base to support the US Army's Task Force Hawk and international humanitarian aid efforts in the Balkan country *(US DoD/JCC(D))*

French *Armée de l'Air* C.160 Transalls were regular visitors to Albania's Rinas airport, which was rebuilt by NATO engineers to sustain the huge volume of traffic that used the airport during the refugee crisis *(US DoD/JCC(D))*

French Army Light Aviation (ALAT) Aerospatiale SA 330 Puma helicopters were heavily involved flying humanitarian aid from Rinas up to refugee camps on the border with Kosovo *(Tim Ripley)*

The United Arab Emirates Air Force deployed four Aerospatiale SA 330 Pumas which were dispatched to Rinas airport in Albania in April 1999 to join the helicopter airlift of aid to border refugee camps *(Tim Ripley)*

The UNHCR employed Ukrainian Army Aviation Mil Mi-8 helicopters to move its aid workers around Albania, bypassing the country's terrible road infrastructure *(Tim Ripley)*

The British Ministry of Defence charted several Antonov An-124 aircraft from Russian and Ukrainian companies to move heavy military equipment to Macedonia

By the end of April the US Army had some eight Boeing CH-47D Chinooks and 23 UH-60A Blackhawk transport helicopters on the ground at Rinas, alongside its initial force of 24 AH-64As. With these additional helicopters the US Army was ready to begin preparing to move up country to take the war to the Serbs in earnest. President Clinton, on advice from his top military commanders in the Pentagon, refused to clear Task Force Hawk for action fearing more than 50% casualties in the face of strong Serb anti-aircraft defences.

BUILDING THE FORCE

Once it became clear to allied leaders that the Serbs were not going to fold, it was decided to step up the air campaign to allow a dual strategy to be followed, with strategic strikes against Serbia being conducted at the same time as tactical attacks against the Yugoslav army within Kosovo.

More aircraft were made available by a number of nations, with the

majority coming from the United States. The USS *Theodore Roosevelt* was diverted to the Adriatic with its air wing which contained more than 70 combat aircraft and helicopters. The 81st Fighter Squadron with more than 20 Fairchild A-10A Warthog tank busting aircraft was sent to Gioia del Colle in the south of Italy to spearhead the attack on Serb armour in Kosovo. An extra squadron of Lockheed Martin F-16C Fighting Falcons was dispatched to Italy to join the Vipers of the 31st Fighter Wing.

Two squadrons of US Navy McDonnell Douglas F/A-18C Hornets spearheaded the strike effort from the USS *Theodore Roosevelt* *(Tim Ripley)*

Royal Air Force Panavia Tornado strike aircraft carried out seven hour long missions from their base at RAF Bruggen in Germany until a forward base in Corsica could be established *(RAF)*

Rockwell B-1B Lancers, of the 28th Bomb Wing, deployed to RAF Fairford in Britain for strikes against Yugoslavia during Operation Allied Force *(US DoD/JCC(D))*

IAI/TRW Hunter UAVs of the US Army's Task Force Hunter operated from Petrovec Airport in Macedonia from mid-April, searching out Serb targets in Kosovo *(TF Hunter)*

Crucial to the expanded air campaign was the deployment of two Northrop Grumman E-8C Joint STAR radar surveillance aircraft, along with a number of IAI/TRW Hunter and General Atomics RQ-1A Predator UAVs. These gave the Combined Air Operations Centre a much needed real-time surveillance capability in Kosovo.

To expand the scope of the strategic air campaign another dozen F-117s were sent to Spangdahlem Airbase in Germany, from where they launched nightly missions against strategic targets in Serbia, alongside F-16CGs operating from the base. British BAe Tornado GR1s based at RAF Bruggen, in Germany, and USAF McDonnell Douglas F-15E Strike Eagles based at RAF Lakenheath, in Britain, also joined the offensive from their home bases. Until Slovakia opened its airspace to NATO in early April, the aircraft based in the UK and Germany had to make seven or eight hour long journeys over France and Italy to reach the theatre of operations.

Throughout the first three weeks of April the F-117s and USAF F-15Es, along with USAF Conventional Air Launched Cruise Missiles and US Navy Tomahawk Land Attack Missiles, struck at a growing number of targets around Belgrade and other major Serb cities. Northrop Grumman B-2 Spirit bombers joined this effort, flying missions from their home base in Missouri to drop more than 600 GPS guided Joint Direct Attack Munitions (JDAMS)s. Military and police headquarters, oil refineries and storage sites, key bridges over the River Danube, Milosevic's residences, political headquarters, television stations and transmitters and industrial sites owned by important supporters of the regime were all targets. Cruise missiles, JDAMs and television guided munitions, such as the GBU-15 and AGM-130, were the weapons of choice for these attacks. They were generally carried out with great precision, although there were inevitably accidents that led to the deaths of

USAF ground crew pre-flight a Lockheed Martin F-16CJ Fighting Falcon armed with a AGM-88 HARM anti-radar weapons, AIM-120 AMRAAM and AIM-9 Sidewinder missiles *(US DoD/JCC(D))*

civilians. During April these attacks gathered momentum and graphic television footage from Belgrade showed a growing level of destruction of key infrastructure targets which some commentators valued at more $10 billion. The political sensitivity of these attacks led to them having to be authorised on a daily basis by senior allied leaders such as US President Bill Clinton and British Prime Minister Tony Blair.

The attacks on Belgrade were at the centre of a major debate about the strategy and tactics of the air campaign, between Short in Italy and his superior, Clark, and a number of allied governments. Short wanted an all out effort to destroy 'strategic' targets deep inside Yugoslavia to apply maximum pressure on the Belgrade regime. It was hoped that the morale of the regime and the Yugoslav people would buckle as the 'lights went off' in Belgrade and other cities as NATO air strikes systematically put the country's electricity grid out of action. Attacks on industrial sites linked with key supporters of the Milosevic regime were also aimed at undermining support for the Kosovo war among the ruling elite.

Northrop Grumman B-2A Spirit stealth bombers flew nightly missions against Yugoslavia from their home base in Missouri during the conflict, refuelling several times during the long flights across the Atlantic *(US DoD/JCC(D))*

The strategy was deeply controversial. Washington and allied governments were sceptical that attacks on so-called 'dual use' targets, such as power plants, were legal under the rules of war, because they could be classed as 'civilian' targets. While maintaining public support for American strikes on Belgrade, the British and French governments quietly ordered their air forces not to bomb any targets in Belgrade. The Americans decided to press ahead with the strikes on Belgrade, no matter what its allies thought. Separate 'US eyes only' facilities in the Combined Air Operations Centre planned and directed the US strikes on Belgrade. Attacks by B-2 bombers were directed from the Pentagon in Washington DC, with minimal involvement by the Combined Air Operations Centre.

The bombing of the Chinese Embassy in Belgrade on 5 May highlighted the divisions between Washington and its European allies. The attack by a B-2 came as a surprise to London, Paris, Bonn, Brussels and many personnel in the Combined Air Operations Centre. According to a Clinton administration spokesmen the attack was the result of a 'foul-up' in the Central Intelligence Agency (CIA) and the Defense Intelligence Agency (DIA), and the use of out of date maps.

Royal Air Force Panavia Tornado strike aircraft equipped with TIALD designator pods carried out daily raids on Yugoslavia *(RAF)*

Since the attack, speculation has been rife about the true reasons behind the strike which devastated the Embassy, killing three Chinese staff. Two theories have been advanced for why President Clinton would have authorised the attack. First that the Embassy was being used as a communications link for the Serb paramilitary leader, Arkan. Second, is that the Chinese were using surveillance equipment inside the Embassy to track US stealth aircraft.

Similar disputes existed between the allies over the imposition of a naval embargo of Yugoslavia. NATO's lawyers told their governments that without a UN Security Council resolution, there was no legal authority to seize Serb ships, because a 'state of war' did not formally exist. Large naval forces, backed by US and Dutch Lockheed P-3 Orion patrol aircraft, kept watch on the Yugoslav navy but it stayed in port, after Clark threatened to sink any warships or submarines that put to sea. Civil shipping was not interrupted.

NATO governments were constantly pressing Clark to step-up direct attacks on Yugoslav troop and police units in Kosovo that were spearheading the ethnic cleansing campaign. Short strongly disagreed with this idea, believing that the main emphasis of the campaign should be against what he called 'the head of the snake'. Clark overruled his air commander and a significant portion of NATO's air power was diverted to attack Yugoslav forces in Kosovo, achieving questionable results.

During May, the additional airpower requested by Clark gradually came on line until some 912 aircraft were arrayed against Yugoslavia, including 355 attack aircraft and 228 tankers. Some 600 of these aircraft were American. The Combined Air Operations Centre staff had grown to more than 1,400 people from 13 allied nations, who were daily schedulling between 500 and 1,000 sorties.

TANKER FORCE

A massive NATO air refuelling fleet of around 200 aircraft was deployed in eight countries to support the Operation Allied Force bombing offensive against Yugoslavia. The tanker operation – the biggest since the 1991 Gulf War – was central to all allied air operations against Serbia. At the peak of the air offensive in May, NATO tankers maintained 15 orbits or tanker tracks around the clock over the Adriatic, Bosnia, Hungary, Albania and Macedonia.

NATO tankers supported air strikes from more than 15 bases in Germany, Greece, France, Italy, Hungary, Spain, the United Kingdom and

Boeing KC-135R Stratotanker aircraft from a variety of units were drafted to RAF Fairford, in Britain, to support the bomber force at the base *(US DoD/JCC(D))*

the United States. Some 175 of the tankers were McDonnell Douglas KC-10As and Boeing KC-135E/Rs provided by the USAF, Air Force Reserve and Air National Guard, with the remainder being contributed by Britain, France, Italy, the Netherlands and Spain. These included Tristars, VC-10Ks, KC-135FRs, Boeing 707TTs, KDC-10s and KC-130s. 'There were airplanes everywhere' said one senior NATO

Royal Air Force Lockheed Tristar air-to-air refuelling tankers passed fuel to aircraft of many allied air forces throughout Operation Allied Force. Here a Luftwaffe Panavia Tornado takes on fuel *(DASA)*

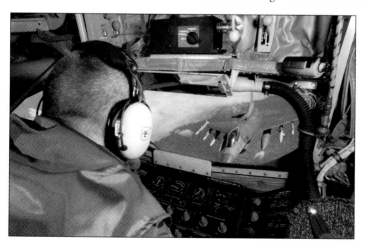

A boom operator of a Boeing KC-135R Stratotanker prepares to pass fuel to a fighter in a refuelling 'track' over Bosnia *(US DoD/JCC(D))*

tanker planner. 'Their location was driven by the need to park airplanes'.

All tanker operations in support of the Kosovo campaign were co-ordinated from the Combined Air Operations Centre at Vicenza. 'It was a challenge building the tanker plan' said Lieutenant Colonel Tom Stark, commander of the USAF 99th Expeditionary Air Refuelling Squadron, temporarily based at Naval Air Station Sigonella, on Sicily. 'It started at the Combined Air Operations Centre with the planners there. They had a tanker planning cell that built the Air Tanking Order and a tanker execution cell that made it happen. At unit level it was very dynamic, especially in an operation as big as this' said Colonel Stark. 'As soon as things started changing - planes started breaking, the weather came in – then that is when the executors in the Combined Air Operations Centre had to keep abreast of things.'

The tanker detachment at Sigonella had around 200 people and a dozen KC-135R aircraft available, and they flew daily missions to supply aircraft to fill a number of tanker 'tracks' positioned in friendly airspace around Yugoslavia. 'We provided in-flight refuelling to enable the strike packages to do their job' said Colonel Stark. 'If we had not been up on pre-strike and post-strike refuelling for the fighters, they would not be able to get bombs on target. We passed fuel to every type of allied aircraft out there with an air-to-air refuelling capability. "No one kicks ass without tanker gas" is the unofficial motto of the tanker force.'

Because we were the closest [US] tanker base to theatre of operations the majority, if not all, of our missions were focused on tactical fighters' said Colonel Stark. 'We also had an alert commitment here to be able to be airborne at short time to provide fuel for alert combat search and rescue effort. We launched when the F-117 and F-16 went down because of our proximity. The F-117 recovery was particularly exciting, we got the pilot picked up. We provided fuel to the aircraft that made that happen. The aircrew here had great

65

pride in that. We also launched to cover for tankers that broke down at other locations further away in France, Spain and England' he said. 'We did over 10% of the cover for other tankers that couldn't get airborne or broke down when airborne. It was a side benefit to our alert duty.'

KILL BOXES

To destroy the Serb army in Kosovo the Combined Air Operations Centre had to create from scratch a system for finding and locating targets on a fast moving and chaotic battlefield. This was a classic battlefield air interdiction effort and the time proven tactic of using 'kill boxes' was dusted off again. Kosovo was divided up into a series of kill boxes, or engagement zones, as they had be called for public relations reasons. Each active kill box was assigned an Airborne Forward Air Control aircraft, usually an Aviano F-16, a Spangdahlem A-10A or a Grumman F-14 Tomcat off the *Roosevelt*. It was the Airborne Forward Air Control's job to patrol over his kill box looking for targets. Once he found a target he would ask the Lockheed EC-130 Airborne Battlefield Command and Control Centre aircraft to get him some strike aircraft that were being held on tankers ready to attack, or on ground alert.

Once the attack aircraft were over the target, it was the Airborne Forward Air Control's job to mark them with white phosphorous rockets or 500lb bombs to allow the 'bomb droppers' to hit their targets on the first run. This system was supposed to give the interdiction effort a dynamic element, to allow NATO to react quickly to sudden movements by the Serb army, but it proved to be a slow business. Firstly the Serb units in Kosovo just went to ground, hiding their tanks, trucks and artillery in woods, factories, towns and villages. The bad weather did not help, but essentially NATO pilots were just not able to find targets in any significant numbers.

Fairchild A-10A Warthog tank hunting aircraft prepare to take on fuel before heading for an engagement zone or kill box in Kosovo *(US DoD/JCC(D))*

On top of this, political concerns about civilian casualties meant very tight rules of engagement were put in place. While tanks in the open were fair game for NATO pilots, any targets in populated areas or near refugee columns could not be engaged without clearance from the Combined Air Operations Centre. It had to verify the pilot's initial report by other means, principally UAVs or signals intelligence. Not surprisingly this proved to be a time consuming process, and often meant NATO jets often had to break off their tracks to refuel from tankers, while waiting for the Combined Air Operations Centre to clear them to attack. This gave the Serbs time to disappear under cover again. On a good day NATO pilots reported being able to hit five tanks. By early April, more than 400 tanks

USAF Fairchild A-10A Warthog tank
hunting aircraft and Royal Air Force
BAe Harrier GR7 strike aircraft
shared Gioia del Colle AB in
southern Italy for much of Operation
Allied Force (US DoD/JCC(D))

and 400 other armoured vehicles were estimated by NATO intelligence to be in Kosovo.

HARRIERS AT WAR

RAF Harrier GR7 pilots of No 1 Squadron were in the forefront of Operation Allied Force flying more than 800 sorties, but finding good targets was far from easy. They called Kosovo a 'dead country' of burning but deserted villages.

'It looked just like Bosnia during that war' said a Harrier pilot, based at Gioia del Colle during Operation Allied Force. 'There was nothing moving around at all during the day time.' Apparently the Serb army had just gone to ground in Kosovo, hiding in forests, villages, factories and towns to keep out of sight of NATO surveillance.

'When General Clark got up and said knocking out five tanks was a good day for NATO he is telling it straight. On some days we couldn't find any tanks. We have never seen a real large group of targets' said the Harrier pilot. 'So it would have been nice to get a good target to hit.'

'Half the trouble was the weather' said another RAF pilot. 'We needed to start ignoring collateral [damage] and start smashing targets but the politicians are not ready to do that.'

AVIANO'S BIG WING

'This is the largest single fighter wing ever assembled at one base' said one senior USAF officer at the Italian base in May 1999. 'There were 185 aircraft on the ramp – Navy and Marine Corps EA-6Bs, Compass Calls and ABCCCs, F-16CGs and CJs, British AWACS, Spanish and Canadian F/A-18s, F-117s and Portuguese F-16s. It's phenomenal. Every loop [parking apron] on the base was full.'

Aviano Airbase is normally home to the 3,400 men and women of the 31st Fighter Wing, but the influx of aircraft and people to fight the war more than doubled the base's population to more than 7,000. 'The temporary duty population was bigger than the permanent party presence' according to a base spokeswoman.

Aviano AB in Italy was the forward base of a squadron of Lockheed F-117A Nighthawk bombers which spearheaded NATO air strikes on targets deep in Yugoslavia from the start of Operation Allied Force (US DoD/JCC(D))

'There were some remarkable tight fits, you had to make sure where jets were pointing when their engines were running. Foreign object damage was a constant battle' said one USAF F-16 squadron commander.

VIPER WEASELS

'Along with the 78th EFS we provided SEAD with our F-16CJs' said Lieutenant Colonel 'Boe', commander of the 23rd Fighter Squadron 'We were the first (SEAD) unit here for Operation Allied Force. We provided force protection for the packages in air to air and air to surface mode. We are the "Viper Weasels", we have a unique capability.

'We tactically orientated ourselves so we had 100% sensor coverage over the area [with our HARM Targeting System (HTS)] when the strikers were working their target area. There was Viper Weasel coverage 24 hours a day. When strikers were in a known threat ring of SA-3 SAMs, and SA-6 SAMs in particular, we were covering the threat area – ready to given them a HARM. We arrived before the strikers came into an area, building up the picture prior to them getting close, so they could adjust their routes accordingly. We provided the electronic order of battle of the enemy and in many cases we also provide the air picture as well. When the 23rd Expeditionary Fighter Squadron was on station not one aircraft was shot down. Two aircraft were lost in the campaign, with zero pilot losses.

31st Fighter Wing Lockheed Martin F-16CJ Fighting Falcon aircraft return home to Aviano AB with their bomb rails empty indicating a successful strike against Yugoslav forces in Kosovo (US DoD/JCC(D))

This is the ultimate bottom line of our mission. We did this just by being on station, by firing HARMs or by the [Serbs] shooting at us instead of the strikers.'

SEAD aircraft escorted every allied air strike into Yugoslav airspace but F-16CJ crews reported a significant reduction in air defence activity by mid May. 'If you look at the whole of the area of responsibility, it quietened down a lot' said LTC 'Boe'. 'Less people were shooting back. At the start of the war we flew only at night. We were close to 24 hour operations by late May.

'The bad guys were smart at exploiting their radar systems. As we got better at employing our weapon systems, they also got better at using their systems. There was a cat 'n mouse game going on', said LTC 'Boe', who reported that his squadron alone fired 150 HARMs in the first two months of the NATO bombing campaign.

'We have had some classic "weasel kills" [hitting SAM radars with HARMs while they are actually guiding missiles at allied aircraft] but they were few and far between. Classic kills were hard to come by because the bad guys were smart.'

A flight of Lockheed Martin F-16CJ Fighting Falcon SEAD aircraft, armed with AGM-88 HARM anti-radar weapons prepare to launch for a mission over Yugoslavia *(US DoD/JCC(D))*

RESCUE MISSION

The night of May 2, 1999, was a nightmare for F-16C Fighting Falcon pilot 'Hammer 34'. He baled out of his crippled jet fighter and was hiding in a thickly wooded area trying to conceal his whereabouts from Serbian troops. 'Hammer 34' had just finished a strike against Serb SAM missile sites near Novi Sad in Yugoslavia when an enemy missile exploded close to his jet and made his the second U.S. aircraft downed during Operation Allied Force. He punched out and watched the aircraft hit the ground in a ball of flames as he parachuted safely to the ground. Hammer 34 said he yelled only 'Mayday! Mayday! Mayday!' over his radio before he ejected. That let search and rescue personnel know he was in trouble while preventing the Serbs from keying in on his location. Later, he said, he re-established communications and assured the search and rescue team he was in good condition. He told them he was searching for a better place to hole-up and would check back in about an hour.

Meanwhile, search and rescue personnel swung into action. The Combined Personnel Recovery Coordination Centre at Vicenza redirected four airborne F-16s to support the recovery operation as the ground team simultaneously transmitted critical details of the situation to the pilots. Rescue helicopter pilots scrambled. The control centre relayed a weather report for the area where the pilot was trapped behind enemy lines – fairly decent with scattered clouds at 10,000 feet and a full moon.

Yugoslav Army short range air defences, such as this SA-9 Gaskin missile system, forced NATO aircraft to operate at medium to high altitudes

When Hammer 34's F-16 crashed, search and rescue helicopter crews were sitting miles away in Tuzla playing cards and listening to radio news about the air war.

'We heard over the radio that an aircraft had been downed and the wreckage had been confirmed in Serbia,' the lead helicopter pilot said. Everybody scrambled to two MH-53J Pave Low helicopters and a MH-60G Pave Hawk helicopter to rescue the pilot before the Serbs could capture him. 'We knew as we headed for the helicopters that we'd

be pressing across the border without delay.' Shortly after lift off, someone shot two surface-to-air missiles at the rescue party. 'We immediately reacted and the missiles missed the formation by about 200 feet.' Two more missiles also missed their target. The Serbs were relentless in their efforts to shoot down the helicopters, but the rescuers regrouped and, just as they crossed into Serbia, the Pave Low pilots to the rear saw a missile coming up from behind. The rescuers evaded them, but the Serbs weren't done. As the helicopters entered a valley, Serb troops fired more missiles, which passed harmlessly through and beneath the formation. After about seven minutes of searching for Hammer 34 at the original pick-up position, the pilots received new information. The airborne computers plotted the downed pilot's new location about 17 miles away.

'As we progressed, we received significant small arms fire,' continued the lead helicopter pilot. As his helicopter popped over a ridge, small-arms fire erupted from a two-story building. His gunner fired back and the attack stopped. Shortly afterward, the leader established communications with Hammer 34. 'He was steering us to his location based on the

US Navy SEAL commandos train to disembark from a US Navy Sikorsky HH-60 Rescue Hawk during an exercise on the USS *Theodore Roosevelt* (US DoD/JCC(D))

rotor noise.' Hammer 34 recalled he'd done that hoping the rotors he heard were from friendly helicopters. The Pave Lows passed by him. When the Pave Hawk pilot saw Hammer 34's strobe light, he made an immediate turn to that location. The Pave Lows provided air cover as the Pave Hawk put down in a clearing. Two Air Force special tactics para-rescuemen and a combat controller jumped out the aircraft. Hammer 34 scampered into the open from a treeline and the armed combat controller ran past him to cover his back. As one para-rescueman covered the team with his weapon, the second prepared Hammer 34 for extraction. Gunfire erupted as the four men boarded the Pave Hawk. 'As I got on board, I laid on top of Hammer 34 in hopes to shield him from small arms fire, because I didn't know where it was coming from,' the ground team leader recalled. As the Pave Hawk zoomed for friendly territory, the two armoured Pave Lows manoeuvered into a sandwich formation to protect it. The rising sun greeted the three helicopters, and so did Serb heavy anti-aircraft artillery and small-arms fire. They evaded the intense ground fire and, looking back as they safely crossed the border, saw Serb spotlights still searching the sky for them.

MIG KILLER

On 4 May a Viper Weasel pilot, from the Aviano based 78th Expeditionary Fighter Squadron (EFS), achieved the first USAF F-16CJ air-to-air kill of the Kosovo war when he shot down a Yugoslav air force MiG-29 fighter near Belgrade.

Lieutenant Colonel Steven Searcy, commander of the 78th EFS, takes up the story of dogfight. 'Prior to the shoot-down four of our aircraft were on a normal mission in the central region, heading for a tanker when they got the call from AWACS that an unidentified aircraft was airborne and could they go to investigate. No1 asked No 4, callsign "Dog", if he heard the call, then he pitched back and got the MiG. It sounded like a couple of seconds but it took a couple of minutes.'

The MiG-29 had taken off from Batajnica airbase, near Belgrade, at 12.41pm and was immediately detected by a NATO E-3A AWACS. Two minutes later the F-16CJs were vectored to engage the threat. At 12.46pm 'Dog' fired two AIM-120B Advanced Medium Range Air-to-Air Missiles at the MiG-29 and a minute later he saw an explosion, which coincided with the AWACS reporting that radar contact had disappeared.

'There was cheer in the operations building when we heard that "Dog" was coming back after the shoot down. I wanted to be there when he landed. When he got out of the plane he had one of the largest smiles on the face of a pilot I've ever seen. A photographer was there, but the pilot immediately pulled all the maintenance guys and armourers into the photo to show that it was a team effort. He wanted the whole team to be in the photo. Then everyone went back to the briefing room to see the tape. It was standing room only in there.'

FRENCH OPERATIONS

In mid-May Paris ordered the deployment of 10 Mirage F-1CT attack aircraft to Istrana Airbase in Italy to allow the French contingent to fly around the clock strike operations. Along with seven additional Mirage 2000Ds and Jaguar strike aircraft, the deployment brought the number

of French air force aircraft in Italy to some 45. They included 12 Jaguars and 15 Mirage 2000Ds at Istrana. A further eight Mirage 2000C fighters were at Grosseto Airbase in southern Italy. Super Etendard strike aircraft flew attack missions from the carrier *Foch* until late May.

The detachment commander at Istrana, Colonel Daniel Bisson, said 'the concept was for the Mirage 2000 to work at night and the Mirage F1s and Jaguars fly during the day.'

Matra 1,000lb laser guided bombs, as well as Raytheon Paveway series 500lb GBU-10s and 1,000lb GBU-16s were the main type of weapon used. Dumb or 'classic' bombs were also used by the Jaguars, in conjunction with the aircraft's laser range finder and targetting computer. French Navy aircraft used Aerospatiale AS-10 laser guided missiles to hit 'hard' targets.

Paveway series bombs were popular with the French crews. 'They are easy to use and very precise' said one pilot. 'When we dropped the bombs they went to the aim point.'

Finding targets for their bombs was not easy, according to French pilots. 'The Serbs have dispersed everything' said a veteran Jaguar pilot. 'We have never fought people like this before – it was not like this in the Gulf or Bosnia. We have great respect for the Serbs. We attack targets given to us by the Combined Air Operations Centre at Vicenza. But first, all targets had to be approved by the French government. Brigadier General Jean Patrick Gaviard in Vicenza decided on the military question, then he sent the objectives to Paris to decide or not.'

'Sometimes they said no' said one pilot. 'Three or four times Paris refused permission for us to bomb.' French air crew did not know the reason for the refusal but it is believed to have been due to the fear of collateral damage. These tight rules of engagement applied to fixed targets, but when attacking mobile targets inside Kosovo, such as tanks and artillery, the authority to release ordnance was delegated to pilots.

'If we recognised the target and could drop our bombs safely then we

French *Armée de l'Air* Dassault Mirage 2000D strike aircraft flew nightly laser-guided bombing missions from Istrana, in Italy (*Matra BAe Dynamics*)

could attack' said a French airman. 'If we had any doubt, and these were French rules, because of bad weather and houses in the laser circle or aim point, we are allowed to come back without dropping our bombs. We do not drop every time. If we had doubt we came back.'

ALLIED FORCE ENDS

All through May, Operation Allied Force continued to gain momentum. USAF Rockwell B-1B Lancers and B-52s based at RAF Fairford staged 'area attacks' on Serb airfields and ammunition dumps. Other NATO strike aircraft hit at the Yugoslav military infrastructure in southern Serbia and Kosovo. Meanwhile, F-117s, B-2s and cruise missiles wrought havoc among strategic targets inside Serbia.

In spite of the pounding being delivered by NATO airpower, Milosevic gave no indication of accepting NATO's demands. During May NATO political leaders at last issued instructions to their military commanders to begin preparing plans for a ground invasion of Kosovo. There, however, was no stomach in western capitals for a bloody land war so President Clinton ordered his assistant secretary of state, Strobe Talbot, to open talks with the Russians on a peace plan. Finnish President Martti Ahtisaari and Russian peace envoy Viktor Chernomyrdin travelled to Belgrade on 3 June and, much to everyone's surprise, Milosevic accepted the proposals when Moscow's man threatened to leave him to his fate if he rejected the deal. The deal allowed NATO peacekeepers to enter the province to establish a UN interim administration. Yugoslav troops and police would withdraw from the province but Belgrade officially retained sovereignty. Yugoslav forces had the right to enter the province and guard Kosovo's borders at an unspecified date in the future.

General Sir Mike Jackson, the commander of NATO forces in Macedonia, was instructed to open negotiations with the Yugoslav military to set the terms for their withdrawal from Kosovo. In a series of meetings in Macedonia, the terms were agreed but NATO strike aircraft continued to attack Yugoslav targets until the deal was concluded on 9 June.

British Royal Artillery GEC-Marconi Phoenix UAVs support the NATO ground operation to occupy Kosovo in June 1999 *(Land Command/Media Operations)*

INTO KOSOVO

As General Jackson concluded his talks, NATO countries began mustering the necessary forces to move rapidly into Kosovo as soon as the first Yugoslav troops started to pull out on 12 June. The NATO-led force was dubbed Kosovo Force (KFOR) and was to be commanded by the ARRC headquarters staff.

Prime Minister Tony Blair wanted British forces to be in the forefront of the invasion and ordered the deployment of an airborne brigade and support helicopters to Macedonia in the

73

first days of June. British and allied special forces were also ordered to move into Kosovo to ensure Serb forces were withdrawing to schedule, and key bridges were not demolished ahead of the arrival of NATO troops. British Army Air Corps Lynx AH.7s of 657 Squadron flew the reconnaissance patrols into Kosovo from Macedonia, and an RAF Chinook of 7 Squadron, based at Gioia del Colle, also moved Special Air Service (SAS) regiment patrols from Albania into Kosovo. NATO UAVs also joined this effort, with British Army Phoenix UAVs filming eleven Serb MiG-21s roll out of a cave shelter at the Pristina airport and take off for Belgrade.

The US Army started to move elements of Task Force Hawk in Albania to Skopje to support the invasion operation. The 26th US Marine Corps Marine Expeditionary Unit was also diverted to Macedonia but it was late arriving after Serb sympathisers in Greece removed road signs pointing to the border. Additional French, German and Canadian forces were also soon on their way.

The ground component of the British invasion force was provided by 5 Airborne Brigade, which commanded two battalion sized battlegroups – the 1st Battalion, the Parachute Regiment (1 PARA) and the 1st Battalion, the Royal Gurkha Rifles (1 RGR). They were ordered to Macedonia on 5 June after it became clear that the Russian and Finnish peace deal was going to bear fruit.

A force package of eight Chinooks and four additional Pumas of the RAF's Support Helicopter Force (SHF) were flown out to Macedonia during the second week of June, with a rest stop in Split, in Croatia, to swap over Chinooks with the RAF Flight based there supporting NATO forces in Bosnia.

The SHF first set up its base at Prilep in southern Macedonia, as 5 Airborne Brigade arrived in country ready to prepare for the insertion. 'I set up my initial Headquarters at Prilep' said Wing Commander Wayne Gregory, the chief of staff of the SHF Headquarters in Macedonia. 'Our Advance Tactical Headquarters element located with 5 Brigade near Skopje. It then moved to assembly area at Camp Piper, just to the north of Skopje and did detailed planning from there. We worked with 5 Brigade on Exercise Corsican Lanyard in May, so we had a close working liaison with them and knew their procedures and people.'

A leap-frogging of assets then occurred until on Friday 11 June, when 5 Brigade and the SHF's helicopters were in Camp Piper ready to mount the operation. Fuel had been forward based in bladders, Mobile Air Operations Teams had were on hand to control the operation and the Joint Helicopter Support Unit had more than 100 underslung cargoes and groups, or chalks, of troops marshalled ready to board the helicopters, which were now based in what had previously just been a wheat field.

The loading plan reflected 5 Brigade's tactical requirements – to secure the furthest most part of the Kacanik defile, set up a reconnaissance screen, put in blocking and screening forces on the flanks, establish communications rebroadcast sites on the high ground and place explosive ordnance disposal teams at vulnerable points in defile to clear Serb mines and booby traps.

As final preparations were being made for the insertion operation to secure the Kacanik defile a high drama was unfolding on the diplomatic

British Paratroopers take cover as they prepare to embark on a 33 Squadron Puma on the Pristina road on the day of the insertion operation *(Photo: Kevin Capon/Crown Copyright)*

arena. Russian leaders were furious that they had not been allocated their own operational zone as part of the proposed NATO peacekeeping force. So to create 'facts on the ground', they secretly ordered 200 Russian paratroopers serving with the peacekeeping force in Bosnia to drive, via Belgrade, to seize Pristina airport so further reinforcements could arrive by air from Moscow. Clark and Jackson were determined not to have their plans thwarted by Russian intervention. Brigadier Adrian Freer, commander of 5 Brigade, was ordered to prepare plans for a *coup d'main* operation to seize the airport ahead of the Russians. At Camp Piper on 11 June, the Paratroopers, Gurkhas and SHF crews dropped what they were doing and prepared quick battle orders for the new operation. 'The helicopters were "burning and turning" when the stand-down order came through, 15 minutes before H-hour' said one senior KFOR officer. Allied political leaders called off the operation with only minutes to spare when intelligence reports came in that 5,000 Russian paratroopers were in the air heading for Pristina. 'It was just like the scene from the movie *Ice Station Zebra*' said one KFOR planner. 'Within minutes we could have been fighting the Russians – the prospect was too horrendous for anyone to contemplate and NATO "blinked".' The following day when it became clear that the Russian airborne threat was a 'myth' because less than 200 Russian paratroopers were actually at the airport, Jackson would order his troops to make another attempt to secure the airport. 5 Brigade's Pathfinder Platoon was alerted to move from their hide to seize the airport. A RAF Hercules, from 47 Squadron's Special Forces Flight, was dispatched to Kukes in Albania to pick up an SAS troop and fly them to seize Pristina in a *coup'd main*. Unfortunately the Hercules crashed on take-off at Kukes seriously injuring several of the crew and passengers. A Dutch CH-47 flew a night time casualty evacuation mission to recover the survivors. Meanwhile in the morning gloom at Pristina airport, the Pathfinders found themselves confronted by the Russian contingent, which arrived at almost the same time. A tense stand-off continued until more British troops arrived later in the day.

Back at Camp Piper, the British helicopter crews closed down their engines and the airborne brigade's soldiers returned to their improvised bivouacs. The plan to seize the Kacanik define was back on. H-hour was set for the 5.00am on 12 June. 'We spent the Friday sitting in a field waiting for the operation to start' said a SHF Headquarters planner. 'The aircraft were our home, we slept in them in sleeping bags.'

THE INSERTION OPERATION

'When we knew we would go at dawn we had little sleep' said a Chinook pilot. 'We pitched up early in the morning. We had a briefing and were given our formation numbers and detailed loads. Five Pumas and two escorting US Army Boeing AH-64A Apache attack helicopters, from 6th Squadron, 6th Cavalry (6-6 CAV), were first over the border. I was in the first Chinook of eight, which were next over the border. Before we crossed the border we could see thousands of people in the refugee camps and roads but when we flew across the border there was no one to be seen.'

The defile is almost 10 kilometres long, and the seizure intact of the main road through it was vital to Jackson's tactical plan to push NATO peacekeeping troops rapidly into Kosovo. Although Serb military commanders had promised to allow NATO free access to the road, key bridges and tunnels had been rigged for demolition and no one was taking any chances on rogue Serb elements trying to sabotage the NATO advance. In the end the Serbs offered no resistance.

'My drop was just south of Kacanik' said one Chinook pilot. 'We put 20 guys and a Land Rover with trailer on a road. The gorge was so steep we had to land with the back wheels on the road. A few aircraft put the ramp to 90 degree so the guys could step off onto the road. The road was empty; we didn't see anyone for a long time. It took three and half hours to put all 5 Brigade in. We shifted back and forth, we used the right side of the defile as the route in and the left hand side as the route out. Later in the day we saw the tanks move. It was what we train to do. To be at the centre of all the headlines that weekend was fabulous. It was exhilarating and exciting to be in the world's eye. All we saw as we crossed the border were satellite dishes.'

With the British armour now rolling forward towards Pristina, the famous intervention of Russian paratroops at the city's airport complicated NATO's plans. A small command team from 5 Brigade went forward to negotiate with Moscow's men. In the meantime the remainder of the Brigade was held at Kacanik waiting on events, with SHF helicopters parked on the roads ready to lift troops forward.

Brigadier Freer had soon established good relations with the Russians and it seemed they would allow NATO troops access to the heavily damaged airport. 1 PARA were ordered to prepare to fly forward quickly to secure the airfield, and soon Paratroopers were boarding their helicopters parked on the road. Then out of the blue General Jackson,

British Paratroopers get into 'chalks' as they prepare to embark on a RAF Chinook at Kacanik during the insertion operation in June 1999 *(Photo: Kevin Capon/Crown Copyright)*

Russian Army Aviation Mil Mi-8MTV helicopters were based at Pristina Airport to support Moscow's participation in the NATO led-Kosovo Force (KFOR)
(Tim Ripley)

on orders from Downing Street media 'spin-doctors' in London, arrived at the airport in his personal Westland Lynx AH.9 helicopter, of 659 Squadron, Army Air Corps, to hold a press conference. The Russian commander was furious at not being consulted and any idea of moving NATO troops into the airport was lost. 1 PARA was stood down again.

The following day the SHF was in action again lifting 1 PARA over the British tanks to the heart of Pristina ready to begin the liberation of the city from withdrawing Serb forces. The Battalion's commanding officer, Lieutenant Colonel Paul Gibson, led the operation with a small tactical headquarters and his C Company. By 3.00pm, the Battalion was complete on the edge of the province's capital and after quick verbal orders, patrols of Paratoopers began fanning out to occupy Pristina to a hero's welcome by the city's remaining Albanian population.

ALLIED OPERATIONS

The British were not the only allied contingent to employ airmobility to achieve their objectives during the opening phase of Operation Joint Guardian. The French Leclerc Brigade was assigned the task of securing the north eastern city of Kosovska Mitrovica. On 16 June, French reconnaissance units were within striking distance of the town but fighting was about to break out in a small town outside the city between Albanians and Serb residents. Rapid action was required if a blood bath was to be averted. The Brigade's Army Light Aviation (ALAT) detachment was ordered into action and soon 20 Aerospatiale SA330 Puma helicopters were landing on the far side of the town to deliver two companies of heavily armed Marine Paratroopers. With peace secured, the French now began to prepare for the final move to secure Kosovska Mitrovica.

French armoured units moved into the city during the early hours of the following morning and began fanning out to secure key objectives. Again the situation was tense. Yugoslav troops were in the process of leaving their barracks in the centre of the city, and fighting could have broken out at any time between Albanian and Serb residents. More troops were needed to establish a presence on every street corner, so Marine infantry, of the Regiment de Marche du Chad, were heli-lifted by ALAT Puma into the parade square of the city's now deserted Yugoslav army barracks. This was the last major urban area in Kosovo to be secured by NATO during the mobile phase of its operation. KFOR now moved into internal security style operations to prepare to hand over running the province to the new appointed UN Mission in Kosovo.

German *Luftwaffe* Panavia Tornado ECR aircraft flew more than 500 missions during Operation Allied Force, firing some 236 AGM-88 HARM anti-radar weapons *(DASA)*

'Commander KFOR gave us priorities of operation and took us back under operational control after we chopped to 5 Brigade for the insertion operation' said Gregory. 'We were to support his airmobile reserve, which was a company of Gurkhas. We were on 30 minutes notice to move them and a couple of times when things heated up we had the pilots in the cabs with rotors turning but things then calmed down. We sustained and supported 4 and 5 Brigades, so one of our six Pumas was on standby for casevac/medevac with two Armoured Field Ambulances to move its immediate response team. That helicopter was based in Pristina on a 24 hour basis. We also undertook theatre tasks as issued by Commander KFOR.'

'We co-ordinated through G3 Air Branch at Headquarters KFOR in Pristina' said Gregory. 'All other helicopter assets worked for specific national contingents. We were the only helicopter assets Commander KFOR directly controlled.'

After good relations were at last established with the Russians it was possible to relocate the SHF from Petrovec Airport to a hard standing area on the eastern side of Pristina Airport to improve servicing and operating conditions. They were then joined later in the summer by Belgian Army Agusta A109 liaison helicopters and a contingent of Russian Army Aviation Mil Mi-8 HIP transport and Mi-24 HIND attack helicopters.

CANADIANS

In an unprecedented operation, 408 Squadron of the Canadian Armed Forces, deployed to Kosovo to support the British 4th Armoured Brigade, with eight Bell CH146 Griffon helicopters. The 170 strong contingent, under the command of Lieutenant Colonel Bruce McQuade, arrived in Greece by ship on 6 June and 10 days later they were flying missions into Kosovo.

'We did reconnaissance, surveillance, casualty evauation, general utility tasks, moving commanders around. We flew 30 hours a day' said McQuade. 'We were co-located at first with the RAF SHF at Petrovec and had access to British communications. We then moved into Kosovo to set up a forward operating base there. We had a liaison officer deployed to 4 Brigade's headquarters and he passed messages to us. The Ptarmigan communications link was key to us.

'A lot of our missions were flown under G2 (intelligence) direction – doing reconnaissance with the British Parachute Regiment. They taught us a lot of Northern Ireland tasks. Our crews learnt a lot. Some days the Paras put an officer in our aircraft, to act as an airborne command post to run their operations.'

408 Squadron's helicopters featured prominently in a CNN news report from Pristina, when the global television network were filming a supposedly secret Kosovo Liberation Army training session. The event was interrupted by the arrival overhead of a Griffon loaded with British Paratroopers.

'We have a Nitesun which is a huge arclight and you can put an infrared filter on and use it with night vision goggles. We have video on our first generation Wescam 118 forward looking infrared. Our IRSTA upgrade project is 18 months away, it is a next generation infrared. That is the way to go.'

By the end of 1999, some 40,000 troops were deployed in Kosovo to keep the peace between its warring inhabitants. NATO operations would start to take on a very different character as KFOR moved to prevent the province's two communities from starting the war again. In the wake of the successful move into Kosovo, helicopters had a key role in sustaining NATO forces inside the war ravaged country as they tried to impose law and order. The province was tense as hundreds of thousands of Albanian refugees returned from exile. Ethnic murder was rife as old scores were settled with the Serb population that remained behind after the Yugoslav army pulled out of the province.

KOSOVO - VICTORY THROUGH AIRPOWER?

In the months after the end of Operation Allied Force airpower practitioners and analysts have been dissecting the conduct and outcome of the largest military offensive in Europe since World War Two.

Two questions remain largely unanswered. First of all, why did Milosevic decided to pull his troops out of Kosovo in June 1999? Secondly, there is still little definitive agreement about the amount of damage inflicted on the Yugoslav 3rd Army inside Kosovo.

In late 1999 the United Arab Emirates Air Force's 69th Air Combat Group joined the NATO-led Kosovo Force (KFOR) operating alongside US Army Aviation units at Camp Bondsteel *(Tim Ripley)*

THE BALKANS 1998

General Jackson told a British Parliamentary committee in May 2000 that the NATO bombing campaign alone had not forced Milosevic to back down. 'I do not believe it is sensible to conclude that Milosevic conceded purely by military action', said the General, who praised Russian peace efforts. He said that while strategic bombing of Serbia was beginning to hurt, 'it is a matter of record that the actual damage [in Kosovo] was rather less than the estimated damage. Certainly when we entered Kosovo we did not have to clear away hundreds of burnt-out tank hulls.'

Then reports emerged that NATO bomb damage assessment claims released by Clark of 93 tanks, 155 armoured personnel carriers and 389 artillery pieces or mortars destroyed by bombing were based only on video footage and pilot reports. The results of a USAF damage assessment team sent into the Serbian province shortly after the NATO bombing were less impressive. They found the destroyed remnants of only 14 Serb army tanks, 18 armoured personnel carriers and 20 artillery and mortar pieces.

A series of conflicting reports and figures have emerged since the conflict about the size of Yugoslav forces in Kosovo, and the level of damage they suffered. Until the allied countries release their raw bomb damage assessment data, and the Yugoslav army opens its archives, there is unlikely to be an end to the 'Kosovo bomb damage assessment debate'.

APPENDICES

CROATIAN WAR AVIATION ORDER OF BATTLE 1995

AB Zagreb-Pleso
Transport Squadron, An-2, An-32, CL-601, Do-28
29th Helicopter Squadron, Mi-24D/V
21st Squadron MiG-21bis

AB Zagreb-Lucko
Transport Helicopter Squadron, Mi-8T/MTV-1
MUP Police Aviation Unit, Bell 205/206

AB Pula
22nd Squadron MiG-21bis

AB Zadar-Zemunik
Training Squadron UTVA-75
Helicopter Training Squadron Bell 206B-3

AB Split-Divulji
Transport Helicopter Squadron, Mi-8T/MTV-1
Fighter Detachment, MiG-31bis

Inside Bosnia
HVO Aviation Support Unit, MD-500

VRS AIR AND AIR DEFENCE FORCE ORDER OF BATTLE 1995

Banja Luka International Airport
92nd Air Brigade
238th Fighter Squadron
    5 x UTVA G-4M Super Galeb
    10 x Soko J-21 Jestreb
    9 x Soko J-22 Orao
    ? x Soko J-2 Galeb
92nd Multi-role Squadron
    UTVA-75/66, Cessna 172, Piper PA-18 Super Cub

Zaluzani
111th Helicopter Regiment
    16 x Soko SA-341H/342L Gazelle
    18 x Mil Mi-8

ARMY OF BOSNIA-HERZEGOVINA ORDER OF BATTLE 1995

Visoko/Tuzla
4 x Mil Mi-8/17
1 x Gazelle

Field Locations
2 x UTVA-66
2 x UTVA-75
1 x Zlin 526
1 x Piper PA-18 Super Club
1 x An-2

Based outside Bosnia
Cessna Citation
1 x CASA 212
1 or 2 Lockheed Martin C-130

UN AND NATO AIR ORDER OF BATTLE, AUGUST-SEPTEMBER 1995

BASE	UNIT	No.	AIRCRAFT	BASE	UNIT	No.	AIRCRAFT
CANADA				Avord	ED36	1	E-3F Sentry
Ancona		1	CC-130	Vicenza	EET11/54	1	C-160D
Sigonella	405, 407					1	Nord 262
	415 Sqns	2	CC-140	Evreux	EE51	1	DC-8
				Sigonella/Elmas			Atlantic
FRANCE				Split-DivuljiDet	ALAT	6	Puma
Cervia	EC3/5	6	Mirage 2000C	/Kiseljak	(3 RHC/4RHCM)	4	Gazelle
	EC2/3	3	Mirage 2000K-2	Ploce	5 RHC	8	Gazelle
	EC1/3		Mirage 2000D			7	Puma
Istrana	EC2/33	5	Mirage F-1CR	Ancona	ET2/61	1	C-130H/H-30
	EC3/11	8	Jaguar	Brindisi	EH1/67	3	Puma
Istres	ERV93	1	KC-135R	Mont de Marsan	EB 91		Mirage IV

BASE	UNIT	No.	AIRCRAFT
GERMANY			
Sigonella/Elmas	MFG3		Atlantic MPA
Nordholz	MFG2	2	Atlantic SIGINT
Ancona	LTG61	1	C-160D
Piacenza	JBG32	8	Tornado ECR
	AG51	6	Tornado IDS
ITALY			
Ghedi	6 Stormo	8	Tornado IDS
Gioia del Colle	36 Stormo	8	Tornado IDS
Pisa	48 Brigata	4	G222
		1	C-130
Istrana	51 Stormo	6	AMX
NATO AIRBORNE EARLY WARNING FORCE			
Gelienkirken/Trapani/Previza		8	E-3A Sentry
NETHERLANDS			
Sigonelle	320/321 Sqn		P-3
Villafranca	322 Sqn	13	F-16A
	306 Sqn	5	F-16A(R)
NORWAY			
Tuzla	720 Sqn	4	Arapahos
PORTUGAL			
Sigonella	601 Sqn		P-3P
SPAIN			
Aviano	311 Sqn	2	KC-130
	12/15 Ala	8	EF-18A+
Sigonella	221 Sqn		P-3B
Vicenza	37 Sqn	1	CASA 212
TURKEY			
Ghedi	191 Sqn	18	F-16C
UKRAINE			
Split		2	Mi-26
Zagreb-Pleso		3	Mi-8TV
UNITED NATIONS PEACE FORCES			
(civil contract aircraft)			
Pleso-Zagreb		2	Il-76
		1	Tu-154
		2	Yak-40
		2	Bell 212
		1	Bell 206
Skopje		1	Bell 212
		2	Bell 206

BASE	UNIT	No.	AIRCRAFT
UNITED KINGDOM			
Gioia del Colle	4 Sqn	12	Harrier GR.7
	54 Sqn	2	Jaguar GR.1B
	111 Sqn	6	Tornado F.3
	No1 PRU	1	Canberra PR.9
Palermo	216 Sqn	2	Tristar
Aviano	8 Sqn	2	E-3D Sentry
Sigonella	Kinloss Wing		Nimrod MR.2P
Waddington	51 Sqn		Nimrod R.2P
Ancona	47 Sqn SF Flt	1	Hercules C.Mk.1/3
HMS Invincible	800 Sqn	6	Sea Harrier FA.2
	814 Sqn	7	Sea King HAS.6
	849 Sqn	3	Sea King AEW.Mk.2
Ploce	7 Sqn	6	Chinook HC.2
	33 Sqn	6	Puma HC.1
	3 Regt AAC	9	Lynx AH.7
		9	Lynx AH.9
		9	Gazelle
Split-Divulji	661 Sqn AAC	6	Lynx AH.7
/Gornji Vakuf	845 Sqn	4	Sea King HC.4
Zagreb-Pleso	RAF SHF	2	Chinook HC.2
(returned UK end Aug 95)			
UNITED STATES			
Aviano	7490th (Provisional) Wing		
	31st Fighter Wing		
	494th FS	8	F-15E
	VFMA(AW)-533	12	F /A-18D
	(replaced by VFMA-224 15/9/95)		
	510th FS	24	F-16C
	555th FS	24	F-16C
	104th FG	12	O/A-10A
	42nd ACCS	4	EC-130E. ABCCC
	43rd ECS	3	EC-130H Compass Call
	429th ECS	6	EF-111A
	3rd FS	8	F-16C HTS
	E Coy 502nd Avn Bn	16	CH-47D
	VAQ-130/141/209	2-5	EA-6B
	VMAQ-1/3	2-5	EA-6B
	(EA-6Bs rotated through Aviano on a daily basis)		
Ancona	37th AS Det	2	C-130E
Sigonella	VP-8/VP-62	8	P-3C
Pisa	91st ARS	6	KC-135R
	(Det 2, 100th ARW)		
Istres	712nd ARS(to 31/8)	6	KC-135R

	99th ARS(from 1/9)		
	(Det 3, 100th ARW)		
Bari	HC-4 Det	2	CH-53E
Brindisi	21st SOS	7	MH-53J
	67th SOS	4	HC-130P
	16th SOS	4	AC-130H
Rota/Souda Bay	VQ-2	5	EP-3E
	USNR TDY Det	2	P-3C
Mildenhall	55th Wing Det		RC-135
	351st ARS	9	KC-135R
Fairford/Cyprus	9th RW Det	3/4	U-2R
Capodinichino	86th Wing	2	C-21
Genoa	9th ARS	5	KC-10A
	(Det 10, 100th ARW)		

USS Theodore Roosevelt

(departed Adriatic 12/9/95)

VF-41	F-14A
VFA-15	F/A-18C
VFA-87	F/A-18C
VMFA-312	F/A-18C
VAW-124	EC-2C
VAQ-141	EA-6B

HS-3	H/SH-60F/H
VS-24	S-3B
VQ-6 Det D	ES-3A

USS America

(arrived Adriatic 9/9/95)

VF-102	F-14A
VMFA-251	F/A-18C
VFA-82	F/A-18C
VFA-86	F/A-18C
VAW-123	EC-2C
VMAQ-3	EA-6B
HS-11	H/SH-60F/H
VS-32	S-3B
VQ-6 Det A	ES-3A

Camp Able Sentry, Skopji, Macedonia

7/1st Avn Regt	3	UH-60A

Note: Maritime patrol aircraft (MPA) are tasked for short deployement (usually two weeks) in support of Operation Sharp Guard, the NATO/WEU embargo enforcement operation aim aimed at the former Yugoslavia. US and Canadian MPA are on longer deployments.

NATO/UN AIR LOSSES 1992-95

3/9/92 Aeritalia G.222. 48 Brigata, Aeronautica Militare Italiana. Shot down by heatseeking SAM 17 miles west of Sarajevo. 4 crew killed.

26/3/93 Northrop Grumman E-2C Hawkeye. VAW-124, USS *Theodore Roosevelt*, USN. Non-combat loss in Adriatic. 5 crew killed.

12/4/93 Dassault Mirage 2000C. 5e EC, French *Armée de l'Air*. Non-combat loss during air-to-air refuelling over Adriatic. Pilot rescued.

11/8/93 Lockheed Martin F-16C. 23rd FS, USAF. Non-combat loss over Adriatic, due to mechanical failure. Pilot rescued.

12/2/94 Grumman F-14 Tomcat F-14B, VF-103, USS *Saratoga*, USN. Non-combat loss over Adriatic after mid-air collision with McDonnell Douglas F/A-18C Hornet, also from *USS Saratoga*. Crew rescued. Hornet diverted safely to Italy.

16/2/94 Lockheed Martin F-16C. 526th FS, USAF. Non-combat loss at Portoroz, Slovenia, due engine failure. Pilot rescued.

16/4/94. Sea Harrier FRS.1. 801 Sqn, *HMS Ark Royal*, British Royal Navy. Shot down by Bosnian Serb heatseeking SAM over Gorazde. Pilot rescued.

24/4/94. McDonnell Douglas F/A-18C. VFA-83, *USS Saratoga*, USN. Non-combat loss over Adriatic. Pilot killed.

15/12/94. Sea Harrier FRS.1, 800 Squadron, *HMS Invinvcible*, British Royal Navy. Non-combat loss over Adriatic. Pilot rescued.

1/1/95. Ilyushin Il-76, Bel-Air charter operator. Non-combat loss at Sarajevo airport during landing in high wind. Crew rescued.

26/1/95. Lockheed Martin F-16C Fighting Falcon. 510th FS, USAF. Non-combat loss over Adriatic. Pilot killed.

2/6/95. Lockheed Martin F-16C. 512th FS, USAF. Shot down by Bosnian Serb SA-6 SAM over western Bosnia. Pilot rescued after six days in Serb territory.

21/6/95. SEPECAT Jaguar GR.1. 54 Squadron, British RAF. Non-combat loss over Adritaic due to engine failure. Pilot rescued.

14/8/95. Westland Lynx AH.MK.7. 3 Regiment, Army Air Corps, British Army. Non-combat loss over Adriatic. Four killed and one crew rescued.

29/8/95. Lockheed Martin U-2R. 9th RW, USAF, Non-combat loss at RAF Fairford, UK. Pilot killed.

30/8/95. Dassault Mirage 2000K-2. 2/3e EC, French *Armée de l'Air*. Shot down by Bosnian Serb heat seeking SAM over Pale. Crew captured but released on 20/12/95

FEDERAL YUGOSLAV AIR (JRV) ORDER OF BATTLE MARCH 1999

AB Batajnica

204th Fighter Regiment

127th 'Knights' Squadron MiG-29

126th 'Delta' Squadron MiG-21bis

Communication Flight UTVA-75

Independent Units

353rd 'Hawks' Squadron IJ-22 Orao/MiG-21R

890th 'Pegasus' Squadron Gazelle/Mi-8

252nd Squadron J-22 Orao

Belgrade-Surcin Airport

SUKL Federal Flying Unit (VIP) Yak-40, UTVA-75

AB Nis

677th Squadron An-2/An-26/Do-28

712nd 'Scorpions' Squadron Gazelle GAMA

787th Squadron Mi-8

AB Pristina

83rd Fighter Regiment

123rd 'Lions' Squadron MiG-21bis

124th 'Thunders' Squadron MiG-21bis

Communications Flight Gazelle, UTVA-75

AB Obrva

98th Fighter Regiment

241st 'Tigers' Squadron J-22 Orao

714th 'Shadows' Squadron Gazelle GAMA

Communications Flight UTVA-75

AB Podgorica

172nd Air Brigade

299th 'Swords' Squadron G-4 Super Galeb

239th 'Vampires' Squadron G-4 Super Galeb

242nd 'Eagles' Squadron G-4 Super Galeb

251st 'Puma' Squadron G-2 Galeb

Team Flying Stars G-4 Super Galeb

897th 'Hornets' Squadron Gazelle/Mi-8

Communications Flight UTVA-75

AB Kovin

333rd Squadron UTVA-75

AB Trivat

Naval Squadron, Gazelle

OPERATIONS ALLIED FORCE/ALLIED HARBOUR/JOINT FORCE - ORDER OF BATTLE/BASING EARLY JUNE 1999

Dal Molin AB, Vicenza

HQ 5 ATAF/Combined Air Operations Centre (CAOC)

Lt Gen Mike Short, USAF

Ala.37 (SP)	CASA 212	1

UNITED STATES
Whiteman AFB, MO

509BW/393BS (USAF)	B-2A	6

UNITED KINGDOM
RAF Fairford

2nd Expeditionary Operations Group

2BW/5BW (USAF)	B-52H	11
28BW/37BS (USAF)	B-1B	5
22EARS (USAF)	KC-135R	5

RAF Brize Norton

106/126 EARS (USAF)	KC-135R	12
216 Sqn (RAF)	Tristar	7
10 & 101 Sqn (RAF)	VC-10	14

RAF Mildenhall

100th Air Expeditionary Wing

351ARS (USAF/ANG)	KC-135R	12
100EOG (USAF)	KC-135	16+
55WG/95RS (USAF)	RC-135V/	5

RAF Marham

No.39 Sqn (RAF)	Canberra PR.9	1

RAF Lakenheath

48th Air Expeditionary Wing

492nd FS (USAF)	F-15E	18

GERMANY
Spangdahlem AB

52nd Air Expeditionary Wing

8&9FS/49FW (USAF)	F-117A	12
22FS (USAF)	F-16CJ	24

Geilenkirken AB

52 ACW (USAF)	E-3B/C	5
NATO AEW Force	E-3A	13

Rhein-Main AB

60th Air Expeditionary Wing (USAF)		
6&9 EARS (USAF)	KC-10A	15
72, 74, 91, 153, 171, 173, 196,		
197th EARS (USAF/ANG)	KC-135R&E	36
12 ACCS (USAF)	E-8C	3

Ramstein AB

Headquarters Task Force Shining Hope		
86th Air Expeditionary Wing (USAF)		
37 AS (USAF)	C-130E	18
17 EAS (USAF)	C-17A	12
193 SOG (USANG)	EC-130E	3

Buchel

MFG 3	Atlantique	1

FRANCE

Istres AB

9th RW (USAF)	U-2S	2
145th EARS (USAF)	KC-135E/R	4/4
ERV 93 (FR)	KC-135FR	6

Mont de Marsan

92nd Air Expeditionary Wing		
?EARS (USAF)	KC-135	24

Avord AB

EDCA 36 (FR)	E-3F	3

Solenzara AB, Corsica

No.9&31 Sqn (RAF)	Tornado GR.1/4	10/2
ER33 (FR)	Mirage F1CR	8
ERS1/91 (FR)	Mirage IV	3
EET 11/54	EC-160 Gabriel	1
ERS 1/11	Alphajet	2 (film delivery)

HUNGARY

Budapest/Ferihegy Airport

171st Expeditionary Operations Group		
171ARW/141ARW (USAF/ANG)	KC-135R	10?

Taszar AB

(USAF/ANG)	A-10A	3
Det JSOTF (USAF)	MH-52J/MH-60/HC-130	
332/533 MAW (USMC)	F/A-18D	24
1st Mil Int Bn (USA)	RC12	4

SPAIN

Moron AB

92nd Air Expeditionary Wing (USAF)		
22, 92 ARS &		
319 ARW(USAF)	KC-135R	24
305 AMW	KC-10A	12

Rota

VQ-2 (USN)	EP-3E	2

GREECE

NAS Souda Bay, Crete

? EARS (USAF/ANG)	KC-135E	7
VQ-2 (USN)	EP-3E	1

TURKEY

Bandirma AB

4th Air Expeditionary Wing		
4 FW (USAF)	F-15E	12
20EFS (USAF)	F-16CJ	12
? EAS (USAF)	C-130	4

Incirlik AB

39th Air Expeditionary Wing		
141 EARS	KC-135E	2
132 EARS	KC-135E	3

ITALY

Aviano AB

31st Air Expeditionary Wing (USAF)		
VMAQ-1/2/4 (USMC)	EA-6B	15
VAQ-132/134/138/140/209 (USN)	EA-6B	10
49FW (USAF)	F-117A	12
494EFS (USAF)	F-15E	26
78EFS (USAF)	F-16CJ	24
510FS (USAF)	F-16CG	18
555FS (USAF)	F-16CG	18
23EFS (USAF)	F-16CJ	24
41/43 ECS (USAF)	EC-130H	2
42 ACCS (USAF)	EC-130E ABCCC	5
145 EARS (USAF)	KC-135	2
No.425/433 Sqn (RCAF)	CF-18	21
No.201 Sqn (PO)	F-16A/B	7
Ala.12/122Sqn (SP)	EF-18	6
Ala.31/312 Sqn (SP)	KC-130H	1
No.8/23 Sqn (RAF)	E-3D	2

Bari Airport

VMGR-252 (USMC)	KC-130F/R	2
HC-4 (USN)	CH-53E	2

NAS Sigonella

VP-10 (USN)	P-3C-III(AIP)	13
HC-4 (USN)	CH-53E	33
AFSOUTH (USN)	VP-3A	1
VRC-40 (USN)	C-2A	4
9RW/99RS (USAF)	U-2S	3
99th ARS (USAF)	KC-135	10
VR-52 (USN)	C-9	1
320/321 Sqn (NL)	P-3C	1
41 Stormo	Atlantique	1

Cervia

53EFS (USAF)	F-15C	5
493EFS (USAF)	F-15C	18
8 Stormo(IT)	F-104ASA	4

Giolle Del Colle AB

36 Stormo (IT)	Tornado IDS/ECR	12
36 Stormo (IT)	Tornado F3	8
No.1 (F) Sqn (RAF)	Harrier GR.7	16
40th Expeditionary Operations Group (USAF)		
81EFS (USAF)	A/OA-10A	18
23FG/76EFS (USAF)	A/OA-10A	4

Brindisi AB/Taszar AB Hungary/Tuzla AB Bosnia

Joint Special Operations Task Force

16SOS (USAF)	AC-130U	3
67SOS (USAF)	MC-130H/P	3
???	HC-130	2
21SOS/16SOW/352SOG (USAF)	MH-53J	9
??SOS (USAF)	MH-60G	4
??	HH-60G	4
193 SOS (USAF)	EC-130E	2

Falconara Airport, Ancona

No.101 Sqn (RAF)	VC-10	5
No.216 Sqn (RAF)	Tristar K.1	2

Trapani AB, Italy

NATO AEW Force	E-3A	4
104th Expeditionary Operations Group (USAF/ANG)		
104, 110, 124FW	A-10A	18

Amendola AB

10WG (BE)	F-16A/AM	20
No.315 Sqn (NL)	F-16A/F-16AM	16
No.334 Sqn (NL)	KDC-10	2
4/9/37 Stormo (IT)	F-104ASA	12
32/51Stormo (IT)	AMX	12

Grazzanise AB

Esk.730 (DK)	F-16A/B	7
331/334/338Skv (NO)	F-16A/B	6
335Skv (NO)	C-130H	1

Grosseto AB

EC 1/5 & 2/2 (FR)	Mirage 2000C	8

Istrana AB

EC7 (FR)	Jaguar A	12
EC3 (FR)	Mirage 2000D	15
EC30 (FR)	Mirage F1CT	10
51 Stormo (IT)	AMX	8

Piacenza AB

JBG32(GE)	Tornado ECR	8
AKG51 (GE)	Tornado IDS	6
51 Stormo (IT)	Tornado ECR	6

Pratica di Mare AB

14 Stormo (IT)	B.707/T	1
51 Sqn (RAF)	Nimrod R.1	2

Brescia-Ghedi AB

181/182 Filo (TU)	F-16C/D	11

Naples – Caodinichino

86AW (USAF)	C-21	2
1st Mil Int Bn (USA)	RC12	5
VR-53 (USN)	C-130T	2
Czech AF	An-26	1
46 Brigata (IT)	G.222	1
Portuguese AF	C-130	1

SFOR - BOSNIA & HERZEGOVINA

Headquarters, The Residency, Sarajevo

General Montgomery Meigs

Tuzla AB

401st EABG (USAF)		
11th RS (USAF)	RQ-1A Predator	
Det JSOTF (USAF)	MH-52J/MH-60/HC-130	

Sarajevo Airport

Commander SFOR Flight (USA)

2 x UH-60L (USA)

1 x C-12 (USA)

Comanche Base, Tuzla

1st Cavalry Division (Forward), 4th Aviation Brigade (US)
A & C Company, 1st Battalion, 4th Aviation Regiment (USA)
24 x AH-64A
D& E Company, 1st Squadron, 7th Cavalry
16 x OH-58D
1st Battalion, 159th Aviation Regiment (USA)
24 x UH-60A/L
4 x EH-60A

'Blue Factory', Tuzla

Medical Company (USA)
15 x UH-60A/L

Metal Factory, Banja Luka

British Aviation Squadron- Banja Luka, Gornji Vakuf, Split
669 Sqn, AAC (UK),
11 x Lynx AH.7, 4 x Gazelle AH.1

Divulje Barracks, Split

Support Helicopter Force (UK)
7 & 18 Sqn, RAF, 3 x Chinook HC.2
845 NAS, 2x Sea King HC.4

Ljubija

322 Sqn (Czech), 2 x Mil Mi-8

Sisava

Viper Flight, Royal Netherlands Air Force
2 x MBB Bo105

Ploce, Croatia

Detachment ALAT (FR),
3 x AS532UL Cougar
4 x SA341 Gazelle
2 x SA530 Puma (Rajlovac)

Rajlovac

Heersfliegerregiment 15 (GE)
7 x CH-53G Sea Stallion
Italian Army Aviation Det
2 x AB205A-1/2 x AB212

Ortijes

Spanish Army Aviation Detachment
3 x AS532UL Cougar

ALBANIA

Task Force Hawk (USA)

Lt Gen John Hendrix

Rinas Airport, Tirana

12th Avn Brigade Col Jeff Scholoesser

2-6 Cav/11th Avn Regt	AH-64A	12
6-6 Cav/11th Avn Regt	AH-64A	12
C&D Company, 5/158thAvn Regt	UH-60L	12
A Company, 5/158 Avn Regt	UH-60A/C	5
159th Medical Company	UH-60A	6
F Coy 1/159th Avn Bn	CH-47D	8
1/229th Avn Regt (82nd AB Div)	AH-64A	12 (not deployed)

ALBANIA FORCE/NATO AMF

Headquarters, Durres
Lt Gen John Reith

Rinas Airport, Tirana

Ukraine	Mi-8	1
Swiss	Super Puma	2
Austria	AB212	4
UAE	Puma	4
Greek (2TEAS)	CH-47	1
ICRC	Puma	1
1 RHC(FR)	Puma	6
15 Stormo (IT)	HH-3F	3
Civil Protection (IT)	A109	1
No 298 Sqn (NL)	CH-47D	2

MACEDONIA

ACE Rapid Reaction Force

Lt Gen Mike Jackson

Petrovec Airport, Macedonia

A Coy, 15 Mil Int Bn (USA) Hunter UAV		6
No 27 Sqn (RAF)	Chinook	8
No 33 Sqn (RAF)	Puma	6
657 Sqn AAC(UK)	Lynx AH7	
659 Sqn AAC (UK)	Lynx AH9	4
22 Battery, RA (UK)	Pheonix UAV	1
RHC (FR)	Puma	2
	Gazelle	4
4 RHCM(FR)	Puma/Horizon radar	2
EH 1/67 (FR)	Puma	2
7th Corps Avn Regt (IT)	A-129	15
	AB-412	2
	Mirach UAV (IT)	
No 298 Sqn (NL)	CH-47D	1

Tetevo

100th Drone Coy (GE)	CL-289 UAV	

Kumanovo

61st Artillery Regiment (FR) Crecerelle		
	CL-289 UAV	

AFLOAT

USS *Theodore Roosevelt*/CVW-8(US)

VF-14	F-14A	14
VF-41	F-14A	14
VFA-15	F/A-18C	12
VFA-87	F/A-18C	12
VFQ-141	EA-6B	4
VS-24	S-3B	8
VAW-1	E-2C	5
VRC-40 Det	C-2A	2 Bari
HS-3	SH-60F/HH-60H	6

USS *Kearsage* (US)

26th MEU		
HMM-365(REIN)		
VMA-231	AV-8	8
HMM-365	CH-46E	12
	CH-53E	4
	AH-1W	4
	UH-1N	2

USS *Inchon* (US)

MH-14/15	MH-53E	10
HC-8	HH-46D	2

USS *Ponce* (US)

VC-6	RQ-2A Pioneer UAV

FNS *Foch* (FR)

11F	Super Etendard	14
16F	Etendard IVP	4
33S	SA321	3

HMS *Invincible* (UK)

800 Sqn	Sea HarrierFA2	7
814 Sqn	Sea King HAS6	7
849 Sqn	Sea King AEW2	2

RFA *Argus* (UK)

814 Sqn	Sea King HAS6	3

***Guseppe Garibaldi* (IT)**

Grupaer	AV-8B	8
	SH-3D	

NATO AIR LOSSES IN KOSOVO CONFLICT MARCH TO JUNE 1999

Manned Aircraft

27/3/99 Lockheed F-117A, 49FW. Shot down near Belgrade. Pilot rescued by CSAR missions.

26/4/99 McDonnell Douglas AH-64A, Task Force Hawk. Crashed on night time training mission near Tirana, Albani, Crew rescued.

1/5/99 McDonnell Douglas AV-8B.VMA-231. Crashed during final approach to USS Kearsage. Pilot rescued from sea by helicopter.

2/5/99 Lockheed Martin F-16C. 31st FW. Shot down near Nis. Pilot rescued by CSAR forces.

5/5/99 McDonnell Douglas AH-64A, Task Force Hawk. Crashed on night time training mission near Tirana, Albani, Two crew killed.

11/6/99 Lockheed Hercules C.1. 47 Squadron, RAF. Crashed on take off from Kukes airfield in Albania. 1 passenger injured.

NATO UAV losses during Kosovo conflict

	Combat	Non-Combat
Hunter	5	3
Predator	2	1
Pioneer	2	2? (possibly Combat)
Phoenix	2	0
CL-289 (GE)	5	0
CL-289 (FR)	2	0
Crecerelle	3	0
Total	21	6

NATO AIR-TO-AIR KILL CLAIMS OVER FORMER YUGOSLAVIA, 1993-99

Date	Time	Type	Unit	Location
1. 28/2/94	0545	G-2 Galeb.	ARSK Air Force	Central Bosnia
2. 28/2/94	0545	G-2 Galeb.	ARSK Air Force	Central Bosnia
3. 28/2/94	0545	G-2 Galeb.	ARSK Air Force	Central Bosnia

All claimed by F-16C 526th FS, USAF flown by Maj Bob Wright. Kill no.1 was claimed with a AIM-120 AMRAAM and no.2 and no.3 were claimed with AIM-9 Sidewinders.

4. 28/2/94	0545	G-2 Galeb.	ARSK Air Force	Central Bosnia

claimed by F-16C 526th FS callsign Knight 25 firing AIM-9

5. 24/3/99	2052	MiG-29	127 Sqn JRV	Near Belgrade

claimed by F-16A of 332nd Sqn RNLAF firing a AIM-120

6. 24/3/99	PM	MiG-29	127 Sqn JRV	Over Kosovo

claimed by F-15C 439th FS, USAF piloted by Col Cesar 'Rico' Rodriguez firing AIM-120

7. 24/3/99	PM	MiG-29	127 Sqn JRV	Near Belgrade

claimed by F-15C 439th FS, USAF firing AIM-120

8. 26/3/99	PM	MiG-29	127 Sqn JRV	Near Tuzla, Bosnia

claimed by F-15C 439th FS, USAF callsign Claw firing AIM-120

9. 26/3/99	PM	MiG-29	127 Sqn JRV	Near Tuzla, Bosnia

claimed by F-15C 439th FS, USAF callsign Boomer firing AIM-120

10. 20/5/99	1246	MiG-29	127 Sqn JRV	Near Belgrade

claimed by F-16CJ 78th EFS, USAF, callsign Dog firing AIM-120

OPERATION ALLIED FORCE MUNITION DATA

Weapon	Country							
	CAN	Fr	GE	IT	NL	UK	US	NATO
LGB	361							
GBU-10								
UK Paveway III						18		
GBU-12								
GBU-16		187		79+				
UK Paveway II						226		
GBU-10/12					286			
GBU-24								
GBU-28								
GBU-15								
MATRA LGB		127						
Missiles								
Maverick					32		800+	
HARM			236	115			300+	
AIM-120					1		8	
AGM-130								
TLAM						20	216	
ALCM							75	
AS-30L		6						
ALARM						6		
HAVE NAP							2	
JSOW							55	
SLAM-ER							?	
Bombs								
CBU-87/Rockeye					165		570	
RBL-755						531		
1,000lbUK						230		
Mk 82	171	128		517			11,000(B-52/B-1)	
Mk 84							20(B-52/B-1)	
Mk82/84					221			
SAMPT 500lb		270						
JDAM							656	
Opher				39				
Others								
30mm Cannon							30000	
TOTALS*		**718**			**705**	**1011**		**23614**

* **Information incomplete. Published figures only.**

COLOUR PLATES

1

Mikoyan MiG-29, Serial Number: 18114, 127th 'Knights' Fighter Squadron, Jugoslaensko Ratno Vazduhoplovsto (JRV) (Yugoslav Air Force), Batajnica Airbase, Belgrade, Serbia, July 1991

The Yugoslav air force took delivery of 14 single seat and a pair of two-seater MiG-29s from 1987 onwards. They saw action in the wars in Slovenia, Croatia and Bosnia between 1991 and 1992, mainly in air-to-ground roles. In the 1999 Kosovo war, 127th Squadron put up the strongest resistance to NATO airpower, losing six aircraft in air combat with USAF and Dutch fighters. NATO claims for aircraft destroyed on the ground during the war seemed to indicate that all of Yugoslavia's MiG-21s were destroyed. At least one has been seen flying since the end of the war and it has emerged that the Yugoslavs created scores of decoy MiG-29s, which included heat sources, to confuse NATO intelligence.

2

Mikoyan Gurevich MiG-21bis, Serial Number: 103, 1st Fighter Squadron, Hrvatsko Ratno Zrakoplvstvo (HRZ) (Croatian War Aviation), Pleso Airport, Zagreb, Croatia, June 1992

MiG-21 '103' was the third jet fighter aircraft to bear the colours of the Croatian War Aviation, as the newly independent republic's air arm was termed in 1992. Formerly a Yugoslav air force machine, serial number 17167, this MiG-21 was flown to the Croatian airport at Split in May 1992 by a defector. It was quickly painted with Croatian insignia and sent into action in the early days of the Bosnian war. The 1st Fighter Squadron was soon nicknamed the Black Knights, hence the knight insignia on the nose. It also bears the motto, Ostventnik Vukovara (Avenger of Vukovar) in honour of the besieged city of Vukovar. Three years later the Croats had acquired around 40 former Ukrainian MiG-21s and they were assigned to the 21st and 22nd Fighter Squadrons in time for the Operation Storm offensive, to secure Zagreb's control over the Krajina region.

3

Lockheed C-130E Hercules, BuNo 40537, 317th Airlift Wing. Location: Zagreb, Croatia, July 1992, Operation Provide Promise

As international involvement in the Bosnian war gathered momentum during the summer of 1992, Germany-based Lockheed C-130E Hercules transports of the 37th Airlift Squadron, 'The Blue Tail Flies', were the first USAF aircraft to fly into Sarajevo carrying humanitarian aid. As it became clear that the airlift would not be a 'one-week' wonder, the USAF ordered reinforcements to be dispatched to the Rhein-Main based 37th Squadron so it could maintain the tempo of operation required. The 317th Airlift Wing at Pope AFB was tasked for this mission, deploying to Rhein-Main to work alongside the 37th Squadron. The two units mixed personnel and aircraft for the missions to Sarajevo, which staged through Zagreb and Split in

Croatia to pick-up pallets of aid from UN High Commissioner for Refugees (UNHCR) warehouses.

4

Lockheed Hercules C.Mk.1P, Serial Number: XV206, Special Forces Flight, No.47 Squadron, Royal Air Force, Sarajevo Aiport, Bosnia July 1992, UNHCR Humanitarian airlift

The RAF joined the UNHCR airlift to Sarajevo in the first days of July 1992 along side French and US aircraft. No 47 Squadron's Special Forces Flight maintained a single aircraft on Detachment in Zagreb's Pleaso Airport and later at Ancona-Falconara airport, on Italy's Adriatic coast, for just over three years flying daily relief flights into Sarajevo. The Squadron was allocated this task because its aircraft were equipped with special equipment to defeat the heat seeking missiles which ringed Sarajevo's airport. It was also a regular occurrence for the RAF aircrew to have to fire chaff to break the 'radar lock' of radar guided anti-aircraft guns.

5

Mil Mi-8MTV, Serial Number: T9-HAA, Republic of Bosnia-Herzegovina (BiH) Army Air Force, Medjugorje, November 1993

Throughout the Bosnian war the Sarajevo government used Mil Mi-8 helicopters to maintain communications with isolated enclaves behind Serb and Croat lines. Most were bought on the East European black market, including Russian and Czech sources. T9-HAA, which was a formerly the property of the Soviet airline, Aeroflot, was seized by Croatian forces at Medjugorje after it was flown to the town, near Mostar, for an abortive prisoner exchange.

6

Westland Sea King HC.Mk.4, 845 Naval Air Squadron, British Royal Navy, Divulji Barracks, Split, Croatia, September 1994

The white-painted Royal Navy Sea Kings deployed to Divulji Barracks at Split, on Croatia's Adriatic coast in the autumn of 1992 to support the British contingent of the United Nations Protection Force (UNPROFOR). The squadron maintained its detachment at Split for eight years, to support the UN and then NATO troops in Bosnia. Its primary role has been casualty evacuation, although during the early days of NATO's Implementation Force (IFOR) the squadron was involved in force projection tasks flying Royal Artillery 105mm field guns to new firing positions to deter hostile actions by local forces. From December 1995 the squadron's Sea Kings were re-painted with olive green-white 'tiger' stripes camouflage to reflect the new offensive capability of NATO forces.

7

Lockheed Martin F-16C Block 40, BuNo: AF89001, 31st Fighter Wing, USAF, Aviano AB, Italy, April 1994

The 31st Fighter Wing was established at Aviano AB,

Italy, in April 1994 to provide the USAF with a permanent combat aircraft presence in NATO's southern region. During both the Bosnian and Kosovo conflicts the 31st Wing was in the thick of the action, with its 510th and 555th Fighter Squadrons flying a wide range of missions. Two of the wing's aircraft were lost over the Balkans, including Captain Scott O'Grady in June 1995.

8

Grumman EA-6B Prowler, BuNo 161779, Marine Tactical Electronic Warfare Squadron 4 (VMAQ-4), USMC, USS *America,* Operation Deliberate Force, September 1995

Suppression of Enemy Air Defence (SEAD) support for allied air operations over the Balkans was considered essential by senior American commanders, sensitive to political opinion in Washington that losses to enemy fire were unacceptable. The US Navy and US Marine Corps Prowler squadrons have therefore pulled a disproportionate amount of Balkan duty, since the first EA-6Bs were deployed to Aviano AB during the November 1994 Bihac crisis. VMAQ-4 operated over Bosnia in 1995 during the final days of Operation Deliberate Force. They engaged Bosnian Serb air radar sites that illuminated NATO aircraft during October 1995.

9

McDonnell Douglas EF-18B+ Hornet, Serial Number: CE.15-12 tail/15-25 nose, Ala 15, *Ejercito del Aire* (Spanish Air Force), Operation Deny Flight, January 1995

Spain's involvement in UN peacekeeping in Bosnia began in 1992 with the deployment of peacekeeping troops to Mostar. The Spanish air force combat aircraft did not become involved in NATO air operations in the Balkans until November 1994 when a detachment of Hornets was deployed to Aviano AB, Italy. Throughout 1995 the service's two Hornet wings, 12 and 15 Ala, took turns to support NATO. Spanish Hornets took part in the May 1995 air strike on the Pale ammunition dumps, the first offensive action by the service since World War Two. The Spanish pilots were in action again during Operation Deliberate Force later in the year and in Operation Allied Force in 1999.

10

Dassault Mirage 2000D, Serial Number: 3-XB, 3e *Escadron de Chasse 'Ardennes',* of 3e *Escadre de Chasse,* (EC3/3), Operation Deliberate Force, September 1995

The French Air Force's involvement in Balkan operations dates back to early days of the UN deployment to secure Sarajevo airport. Mirage 2000D strike aircraft operated from Istrana AB in Italy during both Operations Deliberate Force and Allied Force, using precision guided munitions, such as the AS-30L laser guided missiles and Paveway series laser guided bombs. One Mirage 2000 was lost in August 1995 on a bombing mission over Pale.

11

McDonnell Douglas F/A-18C Hornet, BuNo 164632, Strike Fighter Squadron 87 (VFA-87)/Carrier Air Wing 8 (CVW-8), USS *Theodore Roosevelt,* Operation Allied Force, May 1999

The USS *Theodore Roosevelt* has seen extensive service in the Balkans over the past decade, first deploying to the region in the spring of 1993 during the Srebrenica crisis. Its aircraft flew some of the first Operation Deny Flight combat air patrols over Bosnia in April 1993 and spearheaded the first strike package to 'go feet wet' over Bosnia on the opening night of Operation Deliberate Force in August 1995. The carrier made a rapid trans-Atlantic passage to join Operation Allied Force in April 1999. Hornet 164632 is painted in the colours of the CVW-8 'CAG bird', the personal aircraft of Captain Dale Lyle, 'Sparky', the commander of the *Roosevelt's* air wing.

12

British Aerospace Harrier GR.Mk.7, Serial Number: ZD437, No 1 (Fighter) Squadron, Royal Air Force, Gioia del Colle AB, Italy, Operation Allied Force, May 1999

RAF Harriers operated from the Italian base throughout Operation Allied Force, flying over 800 missions against Serb targets in Kosovo and southern Yugoslavia. The RAF Harrier detachment grew to 16 aircraft by the end of the war in June 1999. Paveway series laser guided bombs and RBL-755 were the main weapons of the Harriers.

13

Fairchild A-10A Warthog, BuNo 80654, 91st Fighter Squadron, USAF, Gioia del Colle AB, Italy, May 1999, Operation Allied Force

Warthogs were the USAF's main ground attack aircraft during the Kosovo campaign, flying daily missions against Serb army units in the Yugoslav province. The 81st Squadron operated from Aviano AB in northern Italy during the first weeks of the war but was re-deployed to Gioia del Colle in late April to reduce transit times to Kosovo. A composite reserve component wing was deployed to Sicily in May to double the number of A-10As available to allied air commanders. The Warthogs flew some of the most dangerous missions, often dropping down into the targeting 'envelopes' anti-aircraft weapons to spot targets for other allied bombers. One A-10A took a direct hit in one of its engines but managed to make an emergency landing at Petrovec airport in Macedonia, proving the aircraft's reputation for being able to absorb heavy battle damage and still keep flying.

14

Boeing Chinook HC.Mk.2, No. 27 Squadron, Royal Air Force, Camp Piper, Macedonia, 11th June 1999

RAF Chinooks played a starring role in the NATO insertion operation into Kosovo in June 1999. They carried troops of the British Army's 5 Airborne Brigade to seize key high ground along the Kacanik gorge, along which NATO troops had to drive to enter the province. All the aircraft involved in the operation were fitted with full mission defense suites and door mini-guns. The eight Chinooks deployed to Macedonia for the operation bore NATO inverted 'V' invasion chevrons.

15

Mil Mi-24P, Moscow Military District, Russian Federation Army Aviation, Pristina Airport, Kosovo, August 1999

Russian participation in the international peacekeeping effort in Kosovo since June 1999 has been extensive, with more than 3,000 troops deploying to the UN administered province. Helicopter assets based at Pristina airport were used to support the three battalions of Russian paratroops serving in Kosovo, flying convoy escort and reconnaissance missions. The aviation detachment was formed from a variety of units in the Moscow Military District. Many of the pilots and aircrew were veterans of the Afghan and Chechnya conflicts.

16

Bell OH-54D Kiowa Warrior, BuNo 40174, Dark Horse Troop, 1st Squadron, 4th Cavalry Regiment, US Army. Camp Bondsteel, Kosovo, February 2000

To support the 6,000 strong US Army peacepeeking contingent in Kosovo, Task Force Falcon, a strong aviation task force was based at Camp Bondsteel, in south eastern Kosovo. The Kiowa Warriors were assigned to fly reconnaissance missions around ethnic flash points or along the sensitive 'boundary' between Kosovo and Serbia. The helicopter's mast mounted thermal imaging sensors were used to video incidents for later analysis by NATO intelligence experts.

COLOUR SECTION

1

1992. French *Armée de l'Air* C.160 Transalls were the first western transport aircraft to land at Sarajevo to kick start the UNHCR airbridge to the city that lasted for more than three years *(Tim Ripley)*

2

Grumman A-6E Intruder aircraft flew close air support missions over Bosnia in the summer of 1993 from the USS *Theodore Roosevelt (Tim Ripley)*

3

In February 1995 the Royal Navy carrier HMS *Illustrious* deployed to the Adriatic Sea with a complement of BAe Sea Harrier F/A 2s on the type's first operational deployment *(BAe)*

4

A squadron of USMC McDonnell Douglas F/A-18C Hornets, VFMA-251, was embarked on the carrier USS *America* for Operation Deliberate Force, August 1995 *(Tim Ripley)*

5

Royal Navy Sea Kings of 845 Naval Air Squadron moved Royal Artillery guns forward as British IFOR troops moved deep into north west Bosnia during December 1995 *(LA (Phot) Terry Morgan/Royal Navy)*

6

USAF Boeing B-52 Stratofortresses based at RAF Fairford in Britain fired some 72 AGM-86 Air Launched Cruise Missiles at Yugoslav targets *(US DoD/JCC(D))*

7

1999. McDonnell Douglas F-15C Eagle air supremacy fighters of the 493rd Fighter Squadron claimed four MiG-29 kills during Operation Allied Force *(US DoD/JCC(D))*

8

US Army McDonnell Douglas AH-64A Apache attack and Sikorsky UH-60 transport helicopters arrive at Tirana's Rinas airport in April 1999 during the Task Force Hawk deployment *(US DoD/JCC(D))*

9

1999. Grumman EA-6B Prowler jamming aircraft had to accompany every NATO strike package heading into Yugoslav airspace to neutralise hostile radar guided SAMs *(US DoD/JCC(D))*

10

1999. Lockheed Martin F-16CJ Fighting Falcons of the 23rd and 78th Fighter Squadrons based at Aviano AB, Italy, bore the brunt of NATO suppression of enemy air defence effort in the first weeks of Operation Allied Force *(US DoD/JCC(D))*

BIBLIOGRAPHY

BOOKS

Compilation, *Air Forces of Former Yugoslavia 1991-1997: Croatia and Bosnia*, Blue Riding Publishing, London, 1997

Martin Bell, *In Harm's Way*, Penguin Books, London, 1996

Christopher Bellamy, *Knights in White Armour*, Hutchinson, London, 1996

General Janko Bobetko, *Sve Moje Bitke*, Vlastit Naklada, Zagreb, 1996

Yves Debay and Eric Micheletti, *War in The Balkans*, Histories & Collections, Poole, 1993

James Gow, *The Triumph of the Lack of Will*, Columbia University Press, New York, 1997

Paul Harris, *Cry Bosnia*, Cannongate Books, Edinburgh, 1995

Paul Harris, *Somebody Else's War*, Frontline Publication, Haddington, 1992

Richard Holbrooke, *To End a War*, Random House, New York, 1998

Jan Willem Honig and Norbert Both, *Srebrenica: Record of a War Crime*, Penguin, London, 1996

Tim Judah, *The Serbs*, Yale University Press, New Haven, 1997

Sam Katz and Yves Debay, *The Blue Helmets Under Fire*, Concord Publishing Company, Hong Kong, 1996

Major-General Lewis MacKenzie, *Peacekeeper, The Road to Sarajevo*, Douglas & MacKintyre, Vancouver, 1993

NATO Communiqués 1995, NATO, Brussels, 1995

Scott O'Grady, *Return with Honour*, Doubleday, London, 1995

David Owen, *Balkan Odyssey*, Victor Gollanz, London, 1995

Miroslav Prstojevic, *Sarjevo, ranjed grad*, DAG Grafika, Ljubljana, 1994

Tim Ripley, *Air War Bosnia*, Airlife Publishing, Shrewsbury, 1996

Tim Ripley, *Operation Deliberate Force*, CDISS, Lancaster, 1999

David Rohde, *A Safe Area*, Simon & Schuster, London, 1997

Laura Siller and Allan Little, *The Death of Yugoslavia*, BBC, London, 1996

Lieutenant Colonel Bob Stewart, *Broken Lives*, Harper Collins, London, 1993

Bob Woodward, *The Choice*, Simon & Shuster, New York, 1996

ARTICLES

Rick Atkinson, *Air Assault Set Stage for Broader Role*, in *Washington Post*, 15 November 1995

Carl Bildt, *Common Purpose*, in Summer 1998 edition of *Defence Review*, London

Lieutenant Colonel Gary Coward, *Feeding Reptiles*, in 1996 edition of *Dispatches: The Journal of the Territorial Army Pool of Public Information Officers*, PJHQ, Northwood

Captain R.C.Dangerfield, *Operation Storm*, in August 1996 edition of *The British Army Review*, Pewsey

Damir Galesic, *Bespilothnih Letjelica*, in Spring 1997 edition of *Hrvatski Gradist*, Zagreb.

Squadron Leader P.N. Hinton, *An Air War without Front Lines*, in June 1995 edition of *Air Clues*, RAF, London

Squadron Leader M.J.M. Jenkins, *There Are No Air Force Personnel in Bosnia: or so you may think if you read the press*, in April 1994 edition of *Air Clues*, RAF, London

Malcolm McDonnell, *When NATO went to War*, in September 1996 edition of *Reader's Digest*

Silvia Miskulin, *Croatia's Secret UAV programme*, in May 1998 edition of *Unmanned Vehicles*, Shephard Press, Burnham.

Colonel David Nicholls, *Bosnia: UN and NATO*, in February 1996 edition of *RUSI Journal*, London.

Colonel Robert Owen, *The Balkan Air Campaign Study, Parts 1 and 2*, in Summer and Fall 1997 editions of *Airpower Journal*, Air University Press, Maxwell.

Gregory L. Schulte, *Former Yugoslavia and the New NATO*, in Spring 1997 edition of *Survival*, International Institute for Stategic Studies, London.

John Tirpak, *The Chief Holds Course*, in January 1998 edition of *Air Force Magazine*, AFA, Washington DC.

John Tirpak, *Operation Deliberate Force.*, in October 1998 edition of *Air Force Magazine*, AFA, Washington.

Major RJ Westley, *The Last Enclave*, in 1995 edition of *The Infantryman*, ITC Warminster.

DOCUMENTS AND UNPUBLISHED STUDIES

Public Information Office Allied Forces Southern Europe, *Operation Deliberate Force Fact Sheet*, 6 November 1995

Briefing by 5 ATAF LO, *A Bluffers Guide to the Former Yugoslavia*, HQ BHC, 2 July 1994

Indictments of Milan Martic, Radovan Karadzic and Ratko Mladic, International Criminal Tribunal for the former Yugoslavia, 25 July and 16 November 1995

Lieutenant General Bernard Janvier, *Force Commander's Operational Directive for the UN Rapid Reaction Force (RRF)*, Headquarters UNPF, Zagreb, 27 July 1995

Wing Commander Chris Morffew, *UNPROFOR G3 Air/Air Operations*, presentation July 1995

Colonel David Nicholls, *Air/Land Campaign Bosnia 1995*, unpublished study

Lieutenant General Mike Ryan, *NATO Air Campaign in Bosnia-Herzegovina "Operation Deliberate Force" 29 August -14 September 1995*, unpublished briefing

Brigadier General O. van der Wind, *Debriefing Report on Srebrenica*, Dutch Ministry of Defence, The Hague, 30 October 1995

GLOSSARY

AB: Air Base

ABCCC: Airborne Battlefield Command and Control Centre

ACCS: Airborne Command and Control Squadron (USAF)

Aeronautica Militare Italiana: Italian Air Force

AG: Air Group (USAF/ANG)

ALAT: *Aviation Légère del'Armée de Terre* (French Army Aviation)

AMRAAM: Avanced Medium Range Air-to-Air Missile

AOC: Air Operations Cell (UNHCR Geneva)

AOCC: Air Operations Control Centre (UN Sarajevo)

Armée de l'Air: French Air Force

ARRC: Allied Rapid Reaction Corps

ARS: Air Refuelling Squadron (USAF)

ARSK: Army of the Republic of Serb Krajina

AWACS: Airborne Warning and Control System

BDA: Bomb Damage Assessment

BH: Bosnia-Herzegovina (UN/NATO term)

BHC: Bosnia-Herzegovina Command (UN)

(Became UNPROFOR 1/4/95)

BiH: Republic of Bosnia-Herzegovina (Muslim)

BSA: Bosnian Serb Army

CAOC: Combined Air Operations Centre (NATO Vicenza)

CAS: Close air support

CSAR: Combat search and rescue

EC: *Escadre de Chasse* (French Air Force fighter/bomber unit)

ECMM: European Community Monitoring Mission

ECR: Electronic Combat Reconnaissance

Ejercito del Aire: Spanish Air Force

ELINT: Electronic intelligence

EU: European Union

5 ATAF: 5th Allied Tactical Air Force (NATO)

FLSS: Forward Logistic Support Site

Force Aerienne Belge: Belgian Air Force

HARM: High Speed Anti-Radiation Missile

HRZ: Croatian Air Force

HV: Hrvatska Vojska (Croatian Army)

HVM: High Velocity Missile (UK SAM)

HVO: Hrvatsko Vijece Odbrane

(Croatian Defence Council, Croat militia in Bosnia)

IADS: Integrated air defence system

IFOR: Implementation Force (NATO)

JA: Jugoslovenska Armija

(Yugoslav armed forces, post 1992) (also VJ)

JAOC: Joint Air Operations Cell (UNHCR Ancona)

JAP: Joint Action Plan (US diplomatic plan)

JCO: Joint Commission Observer (UK SAS)

JNA: Jugoslovenska Narodna Armija

(Federal Yugoslav armed forces, pre 1991)

JRV: Federal Yugoslav Air Force

KFOR: Kosovo Force (NATO)

KLA: Kosovo Liberation Army (also UCK)

KVCC: Kosovo Verification Co-ordination Centre

KVM: Kosovo Verification Mission

MCCC: Monitoring Close Air Support Centre (UN Zagreb)

MEAT: Munitions Effectivness Team

MUP: Ministry of Interior Special Police

(term used in all former Yugoslav republics)

NAEWF: NATO Airborne Early Warning Force

NAS: Naval Air Station

NATO: North Atlantic Treaty Organisation

NSA: National Security Agency (US)

NSC National Security Council (US)

RAF: Royal Air Force (UK)

RRF: Rapid Reaction Force (UN)

RRFOS: Rapid Reaction Force Operations Staff (UN)

SAM: Surface-to-air missile

SAS: Special Air Service (UK)

SEAD: Suppression of enemy air defence

SEAL: Sea-Air-Land

SFOR: Stabilisation Force (NATO)

SHAPE: Supreme Headquarters Allied Powers Europe

SHF: Support Helicopter Force (SHF)

SLAM: Stand-off land attack missile

SOS: Special Operations Squadron (SOS)

STAR: Surveillance Target Attack Radar

Stormo: Italian Air Force wing sized unit

TACP: Tactical air control party

TARPS: Tactical Air Reconnaissance Pod System

TIALD Thermal Imaging and Laser Designation

TLAM: Tomahawk Land Attack Missile

TRIAD: Tri-Wall Aerial Distribution System

TRW ???

UAV: Unmaned Air Vehicle

UCK: Kosovo Liberation Army (also KLA)

UN: United Nations

UNCRO: United Nations Confidence Restoring Operation

(succeeded UNPROFOR in Croatia on 1/4/95)

UNHCR: United Nations High Commissioner for Refugees

UNMO: United Nations Military Observer

UNPF: United Nations Peace Forces

(succeeded UNPROFOR on 1/4/95)

UNPROFOR: United Nations Protection Force

USAF: United States Air Force

USMC: United States Marine Corps

USS: United States Ship

VJ: Federal Yugoslav Armed Forces (post 1992) (also JA)

VFMA: US Marine Fighter Attack Squadron

VRS: Bosnian Serb Army